PENGUIN PLAYS

ABIGAIL'S PARTY

AND

GOOSE-PIMPLES

Mike Leigh, dramatist and theatre and film director, was born in 1943 at Salford in Lancashire. He trained at the Royal Academy of Dramatic Art, at Camberwell and Central Art Schools, and at the London Film School. After this he gained wide acting, directing and designing experience at various theatres, including a season with the Royal Shakespeare Company. His first original play was *The Box Play*, performed at the Midlands Arts Centre in Birmingham in 1965.

His BBC films include *Hard Labour* (1973), *Nuts in May* (1975), *The Kiss of Death* (1976), *Who's Who* (1978), *Grown-Ups* (1980), *Home Sweet Home* (1982) and *Four Days in July* (1984). His films for Channel 4 are *Meantime* (1983), *The Short and Curlies* (1987), and the highly successful feature films *High Hopes* (1988), *Life is Sweet* (1990), *Naked* (1993), for which he won Best Director award at the 1993 Cannes Film Festival, *Secrets & Lies* (1995) and *Career Girls* (1997). His earlier feature *Bleak Moments* was developed from a play of the same name at the Open Space Theatre, London, and his many other stage-plays include *Wholesome Glory* (Royal Court, 1973), *Babies Grow Old* (RSC, 1974), *Greek Tragedy* (Belvoir Street Theatre, Sydney, Australia, 1989) and *It's a Great Big Shame!* (Theatre Royal Stratford East, 1993).

Abigail's Party (1977) was first produced at the Hampstead Theatre and was later screened as a BBC Play For Today. *Goose-Pimples* (1981), which won the *Evening Standard* Best Comedy of the Year Award, was first produced at the Hampstead Theatre and then transferred to a successful run in the West End. His other Hampstead plays have been *Ecstasy* (1979) and *Smelling a Rat* (1988).

Mike Leigh was awarded an OBE in 1993.

ABIGAIL'S PARTY
AND
GOOSE-PIMPLES

BY MIKE LEIGH

PENGUIN BOOKS

PENGUIN BOOKS

Published by the Penguin Group
Penguin Books Ltd, 80 Strand, London WC2R 0RL, England
Penguin Putnam Inc., 375 Hudson Street, New York, New York 10014, USA
Penguin Books Australia Ltd, 250 Camberwell Road, Camberwell, Victoria 3124, Australia
Penguin Books Canada Ltd, 10 Alcorn Avenue, Toronto, Ontario, Canada M4V 3B2
Penguin Books India (P) Ltd, 11 Community Centre, Panchsheel Park, New Delhi – 110 017, India
Penguin Books (NZ) Ltd, Cnr Rosedale and Airborne Roads, Albany, Auckland, New Zealand
Penguin Books (South Africa) (Pty) Ltd, 24 Sturdee Avenue, Rosebank 2196, South Africa

Penguin Books Ltd, Registered Offices: 80 Strand, London WC2R 0RL, England

www.penguin.com

Abigail's Party first published (in *Plays of the Year 47*) by Paul Elek 1979
Copyright © Mike Leigh, 1977
Goose-Pimples first published by Samuel French 1982
Copyright © Mike Leigh, 1982
This collection published in Penguin Books 1983
18

All rights reserved

Printed in England by Clays Ltd, St Ives plc
Filmset in Monophoto Garamond

ISBN-13: 978–0–140–48180–8

CONTENTS

Abigail's Party   7

Goose-Pimples   71

Notes   156

ABIGAIL'S PARTY

First performed at the Hampstead Theatre, London, on 18 April 1977, when the cast was as follows:

BEVERLY	*Alison Steadman*
LAURENCE	*Tim Stern*
ANGELA	*Janine Duvitski*
TONY	*John Salthouse*
SUSAN	*Thelma Whiteley*

By Mike Leigh
Designed by Tanya McCallin
Costumes by Lindy Hemming
Lighting by Alan O'Toole

In a later revival at Hampstead Theatre (from 18 July 1977), and also in the television version transmitted as a *Play for Today* on BBC-1 on 1 November 1977, Harriet Reynolds appeared as Susan.

Abigail's Party was evolved from scratch entirely by rehearsal through improvisation.

ACT I
Early evening in spring

ACT II
Later that evening

Time – the present

ACT I

Laurence and Beverly's house, the ground floor. Room divider shelf unit, including telephone, stereo, ornamental fibre-light, fold-down desk, and prominently placed bar. Leather three-piece suite, onyx coffee-table, sheepskin rug. Open-plan kitchen, dining area with table and chairs. Hall and front door unseen.

Lights up.

Enter Beverly. She puts on a record (Donna Summer: Love to Love you Baby). Lights a cigarette. Places a copy of Cosmopolitan in magazine rack. Pours a gin-and-tonic. Gets a tray of crisps and salted peanuts from the kitchen and puts it on the coffee table. Sits.

Pause.

Enter Laurence, with executive case.

LAURENCE [*kissing her*]: Hullo.

BEVERLY: Hi.

  [*Laurence puts case on armchair.*]

You're late.

LAURENCE: Sorry? [*Laurence turns down music.*]

BEVERLY: I said, you're late.

  [*Laurence pours himself a scotch.*]

LAURENCE: Yes: sorry about that – unavoidable.

BEVERLY: What happened?

LAURENCE: Oh, some clients, they were late.

BEVERLY: Laurence, don't leave your bag on there, please.

LAURENCE: I'll move it in a minute.

BEVERLY: D'you get something to eat?

LAURENCE: No.

BEVERLY: No? I had to throw your pizza away, I'm sorry.

  [*Beverly gets from fridge two small platesful of home-made cheese-and-pineapple savouries, each consisting of one cube of cheese and one chunk of pineapple on a cocktail stick.*

  Laurence opens desk. Gets case. Opens notebook. Goes to phone.

  Beverly returns, puts plates on coffee-table.]

LAURENCE: Just got to make a couple of phone calls.

BEVERLY: D'you want me to make you a little sandwich?

LAURENCE: No, I must get these out of the way first.

BEVERLY: Laurence, you want to have your bath and get changed: they're going to be here soon.

LAURENCE: Yes.

>[*Beverly sits.*]

>Oh, is Mr O'Halligan there, please? O'Halligan. Yes. Well, he's big. He's bald, with red hair. Thank you.

>[*Pause.*]

BEVERLY: Laurence, you're going to get heartburn.

LAURENCE: Mr O'Halligan? Mr Moss here, Wibley Webb. Hullo. D'you realize I've been trying to contact you all afternoon? I know you've been out! Now, where's that key to 15 Clittingham Avenue? Ah, but you were supposed to have it back before lunch! That's no good, I need it now. Will you be in tomorrow morning? Tonight! Where? Belfast? What time's your plane? All right, train then. A party? I thought you just said you were going to Belfast! Well, what time are you going to Kilburn? Well, what time are you having your bath? I'm not asking you to bath in cold water – I just want the key to 15 Clittingham Avenue; I've got another client who wants to view the property. What about you, Mr O'Halligan? Well, Mr O'Halligan, if you'd like to come in on Monday morning with your deposit, and go ahead and get in touch with your Building Society we'll see how things go. Now what about this key? All right, I will come and get it! Now!

BEVERLY: Laurence – no!

LAURENCE: Yes, I've got the address. Yes, I know how to get there. Okay – I'll see you shortly – Goodbye! [*He hangs up.*] Stupid man.

BEVERLY: Oh, Christ, Laurence.

LAURENCE: What?

BEVERLY: How long's all this going to take, please?

LAURENCE: Oh, yes – I'm sorry. It won't take long. [*He dials another number.*]

BEVERLY: D'you get those lagers?

LAURENCE: Er, no: I didn't have time.

BEVERLY: Laurence! [*Pause.*] Well, you'd better get them when you go out, and don't forget, please.

LAURENCE: Hullo, Mrs Cushing? Laurence Moss here, Wibley Webb! Yes, Mrs Cushing, we have run him to ground, and you'll be happy to know that I'm now in the throes of retrieving the key!

>[*Beverly gets herself another drink.*]

>Not at all, not at all – all part of the service! Ah. Ah, yes ... now, when would be best for you? No, no, I'll fall in with you, Mrs Cushing. How about tomorrow morning?

BEVERLY: Laurence!

LAURENCE: My pleasure, Mrs Cushing, my pleasure. Now, what time would suit you best? No, I'm at your service, Mrs Cushing: he who pays the piper calls the tune! You name the hour, and I shall appear! No, really: I insist. What time? Eight o'clock? Sure, surely.

BEVERLY: Laurence!!

LAURENCE: Early? Not at all, Mrs Cushing – up with the lark, you know. Don't mention it, Mrs Cushing, it's my privilege. 'Bye, Mrs Cushing – see you tomorrow morning! 'Bye now! [*He hangs up.*]

BEVERLY: You're going to kill yourself, you know, Laurence.

LAURENCE: Yes. Well, it can't be helped.

BEVERLY: It's ridiculous.

LAURENCE: It's not a nine to five job – you know that, Beverly.

BEVERLY: You can say that again.

　　[*Laurence sits with Beverly.*]

　　You gonna get changed?

LAURENCE: Yes. I'll drink this; I'll get changed; then I'll go out.

BEVERLY: And don't forget those lagers.

LAURENCE: Beverly; where are the olives?

BEVERLY: In the kitchen, Laurence. Laurence, if you want olives, would you put them out, please?

　　[*The front door bell chimes.*]

LAURENCE [*jumping up*]: They're early, aren't they?

BEVERLY: No, they're not. And you've not changed.

LAURENCE: I know that. [*He goes to answer the door.*] Beverly, get the olives.

　　[*Beverly composes herself, then rises, and prepares to receive guests. Meanwhile, offstage:*]

ANGELA: Hello, you must be Laurence!

LAURENCE: That's right.

ANGELA: I'm Angie.

LAURENCE: Do go in, won't you?

ANGELA: Thank you. This is my husband, Tony.

TONY: How d'you do.

LAURENCE: Hullo.

　　[*They come in.*]

BEVERLY: Hi, Ang.

ANGELA: Hello, Beverly – what a lovely dress!

BEVERLY: Thanks.

ANGELA: Were we meant to wear long?

BEVERLY: No, no, it's just informal, you know, so ...

ANGELA: This is my husband, Tony.

BEVERLY: How d'you do, pleased to meet you.

TONY: How d'you do.

BEVERLY: He's got a firm handshake, hasn't he?

ANGELA: Yes.

BEVERLY: Yeah, fantastic. Like to go through?

TONY: Ta.

ANGELA: This is the suite I was telling you about. It's nice, isn't it?

TONY: Lovely.

ANGELA: We've just bought a new three-piece suite, but ours isn't real leather, like this – it's 'leather look'.

BEVERLY: Oh, the Leather Look? Great.

LAURENCE: Drink?

TONY: Yes, please.

BEVERLY: Laurence, would you like to take Angela's coat, please?

LAURENCE: Surely.

ANGELA: Thanks.

LAURENCE: Pleasure.

  [*Laurence takes coat out.*]

BEVERLY: It's funny, 'cos he's a lot bigger than I thought he was. Yeah ... 'cos I've seen him across the road, Ang, and I thought he was about the same size as Laurence –

ANGELA: Oh, no ...

BEVERLY: – but he's not, he's a lot bigger, yeah, great. Would you like a drink?

TONY: Yes, please.

BEVERLY: What would you like?

TONY: Bacardi-and-Coke, please.

BEVERLY: Ice and lemon?

TONY: Yes, please.

BEVERLY: Great. How about you, Ang?

ANGELA: Have you got gin?

BEVERLY: Gin-and-tonic?

ANGELA: Please.

BEVERLY: Ice and lemon?

ANGELA: Yes, please.

BEVERLY: Great.

  [*Enter Laurence.*]

  Laurence, would you like to get the drinks, please? Tony would like Bacardi-and-Coke with ice and lemon, Angela would like a gin-and-tonic with ice and lemon, and I'd like a little fill-up, okay?

LAURENCE: Surely.

BEVERLY: D'you like lager, Tony?

TONY: I'll be all right with Bacardi, thank you.

BEVERLY: No – as a chaser, a little bit later on; because Laurence is gonna get some.

TONY: It'll be okay, thank you.

BEVERLY: Or a light ale. Which d'you prefer?

TONY: Light ale.

BEVERLY: Light ale? Laurence, would you get some light ale as well, please?

LAURENCE: Yes.

BEVERLY: Actually, Ang, it's going to be really nice, because I've invited Sue from Number 9.

ANGELA: Oh, lovely.

BEVERLY: Yeah, so I thought it'd be nice for you to meet her as well. Yeah, 'cos her daughter's having a party. Well, she's only a teenager, so I said, well, pop down and spend the evening with us.

ANGELA: That'd be really nice, 'cos I want to meet all the neighbours.

BEVERLY: Yeah, just say hello, Ang, and break the ice.

ANGELA: 'Cos that was what was so nice when you came over, 'cos it really made me feel at home.

BEVERLY: Well, Ang, I know what I felt like when I moved in – I was lonely. So I thought, well, that's not going to happen to you.

ANGELA: Well, you're the friendly type, aren't you?

BEVERLY: Yeah, yeah. It's funny, 'cos as soon as we met, I knew we were gonna get on.

ANGELA: Well, we're alike, aren't we?

BEVERLY: Yeah, yeah.

[*Laurence gives them their drinks.*]

Thanks.

ANGELA: Thanks.

[*Laurence gives Tony his drink.*]

TONY: Thank you.

BEVERLY: Cheers, everyone!

ANGELA: Cheers!

BEVERLY: Cheers, Tone!

TONY: Cheers.

[*Laurence gets his glass from the coffee-table.*]

LAURENCE: Cheers!

ANGELA: Cheers!

BEVERLY: What are you doing, darling? Are you staying, or going?

LAURENCE: Er, I'll stay for a while.

BEVERLY: Laurence has to pop out on business, I'm afraid, so ...
Now: anybody like a cigarette? Laurence, would you, please?
   [*Laurence offers cigarette box.*]
BEVERLY: Angela?
ANGELA: No, thanks.
BEVERLY: Tony, would you like a cigarette?
TONY: No, thank you.
ANGELA: We've just given up.
BEVERLY: Oh, yeah. Sorry!
LAURENCE: Now, who'd like some olives?
BEVERLY: Not for me. Ang?
ANGELA: No, thanks.
BEVERLY: Tony, d'you like olives?
TONY: No, I don't.
BEVERLY: No, they're horrible, aren't they?
ANGELA: Yes.
BEVERLY: They've got a very bitter taste, haven't they, Ang?
ANGELA: Yes.
BEVERLY: I told you nobody'd like olives, Laurence.
LAURENCE: Not nobody, Beverly: I like olives. And that's twenty-
   five per cent of the assembled company.
ANGELA: We've met you before, haven't we?
LAURENCE: Really?
ANGELA: He is the one you remember, isn't he?
TONY: Yeah.
ANGELA: D'you remember us? We came looking for a house.
LAURENCE: I can't say I do; of course, we see a lot of clients.
TONY: We saw a lot of estate agents.
ANGELA: Yes, we went to all the ones in the area. We got the house from
   Spencer's in the end – Anthony Spencer.
BEVERLY: Oh, Anthony Spencer, yeah, yeah.
ANGELA: Well, it was Nicholas Spencer who was dealing with us.
BEVERLY: Yeah?
ANGELA: He's very nice. D'you know him?
LAURENCE: Yes, I know him.
ANGELA: Have you seen those boards they have outside?
BEVERLY: Ang, aren't they beautiful?
ANGELA: Yes, they're lovely. With the house and the family and the
   car and the tree. When I saw them I thought, 'I hope we get a
   house with one of those boards.' I expect they sell a lot of houses
   because of the boards. Don't you think so?

LAURENCE: No, actually, I don't.

ANGELA: Oh, don't you? We were very lucky, actually, 'cos we got the price of the house down from twenty-two thousand to twenty-one thousand.

BEVERLY: Really? Oh, that is fantastic, Ang, that's really great.

[*During following, Beverly offers cheese-pineapple savouries to Angela and Tony. So does Laurence, though superfluously as it turns out. Tony says 'Ta' where appropriate.*]

BEVERLY: Is it your first house?

ANGELA: Yes, we were in a furnished flat before.

BEVERLY: Oh, that's a bit grim, isn't it, furnished flat? Yeah.

ANGELA: Yes. Well it was nice for us while we were saving.

BEVERLY: Yeah.

ANGELA: But the trouble is, with it being furnished, it means we haven't got much furniture of our own together yet.

BEVERLY: Yeah, and you feel it when you move, don't you?

ANGELA: Yes.

BEVERLY: Mind you, Ang, your house is smaller than this one, yeah, because I know they are smaller on your side, yeah.

ANGELA: Yes. Mmm. These are lovely.

BEVERLY: Yes, they're dainty, aren't they?

[*Beverly has sat down again.*]

Your bed arrived yet, Ang?

ANGELA: Oh, don't talk about that – it's a sore point.

BEVERLY: Is it?

ANGELA: Well, it's funny, really ... 'cos I came back from work today, 'cos I'm not working nights any more, I'm on days.

BEVERLY: Yeah?

ANGELA: And I came home, and I saw this big parcel in the hall, and I saw his face, and he was looking furious, and I thought, What's happened? ... and you know what? The bed-head had arrived, and no bed.

BEVERLY: No, Ang! Laurence, did you hear that? How many weeks ago is it you ordered that bed, Ang?

ANGELA: Four.

BEVERLY: Four weeks ago they ordered a bed, and it still hasn't arrived. It's disgusting.

LAURENCE: Well, you can't trust anybody these days.

ANGELA: No.

BEVERLY: It's disgraceful. I mean, you've been sleeping on the floor, haven't you, Ang?

ANGELA: Yes. Well, we've got a mattress from Tony's mum, but it's
not the same.

BEVERLY: No. Well, let's face it, Tone, you can't do much with a bed-
head, can you? D'you know what I mean?
[*Pause.*]

LAURENCE: What line of business are you in?

TONY ⎫: Computers.
ANGELA ⎭: He's in computers.

BEVERLY: Oh, really, Tone? That's funny, 'cos my brother's in
computers, actually.

ANGELA: Is he?

BEVERLY: Yeah, he's a ... programmes analyst.

ANGELA: Oh, yes? Tony's, just an operator.

BEVERLY: I know it's a fantastic job, though, Tone, 'cos my brother,
he had to go to college and get exams. I mean, he was studying for
years, wasn't he, Laurence?

LAURENCE: Oh, yes.

BEVERLY: Did you have to do all that, Tone? – go to college?

ANGELA: You didn't really, did you?

TONY: No.

ANGELA: No.

BEVERLY: I know it is a fantastic job, though, Tone, 'cos my brother,
he's got a fabulous house and he gets great wages, y'know?
Yeah.

LAURENCE: Nine to five, is it?

TONY: No, it's not, actually; there's quite a bit of variation.

ANGELA: Shift-work.

TONY: It's a two-weekly system: one week I work from eight in the
morning till four in the afternoon, and the following week I work
from four till midnight. I get every other Saturday off.

BEVERLY: Oh, great. Were you off today, Tone?

TONY: Yeah, I was, actually.

ANGELA: Yes. It's lucky, 'cos if I'm working on a Saturday, he can do
all the shopping.

LAURENCE: Oh, yes? Where do you shop?

ANGELA ⎫:Sainsbury's.
TONY ⎭

LAURENCE: Ah, we usually go to the Co-op: I find they have a much
wider range of goods there.

BEVERLY: Don't you find shopping boring, though, Ang?

ANGELA: Mmm.

BEVERLY: Oh, I do – I hate it. He takes me down in the car, and I get me wheely, Tone, and I whizz in, and I grab anything I can see, and I bung it in the wheely, he writes me a cheque, we bung it in the car, bring it home, and it's done for the week, d'you know what I mean?

LAURENCE: Beverly is not very organized: she doesn't believe in making shopping-lists. You have a car, do you?

TONY: Yeah.

ANGELA: Yes, an Escort.

LAURENCE: A yellow one?

ANGELA: That's it.

LAURENCE: Yes, I've seen it.

BEVERLY: Yeah, it's beautiful, actually.

ANGELA: Beverly was saying you only like Minis.

LAURENCE: No, not at all. I don't only like Minis – I like lots of other cars. But I find the Mini economical, efficient and reliable, and the most suited to my purposes. Of course, I change my car every year.

BEVERLY: Yeah, but what I say, Ang, is this: What is the point of changing your car if all you change is the colour?

LAURENCE: That's not all you change, Beverly; the design does alter. But then you're not a motorist, so of course you just don't understand these things.

BEVERLY: Yeah, okay. I know I failed my test three times.

LAURENCE: Three times.

BEVERLY: But, I'm his wife, Ang, and I reckon a wife should have a little say in the choosing of a car.

LAURENCE: Well, when you've passed your test, Beverly, then you can have your little say. Until then, please leave it to me.

BEVERLY: Let me put it to you this way, Ang. When we chose the furniture, we chose it together; when we chose the house, we chose it together; but, when it comes to the car, I'm not allowed to have a say.

[*Laurence goes.*]

Don't forget those light ales!

LAURENCE: No – and the lagers, yes!

ANGELA: You going to take your test again?

BEVERLY: Yeah, I'm going to have another try, yeah. Don't get me wrong, Tone, it's not that I can't drive – in fact I'm a good driver, but, let me put it to you this way, when I get to my test my nerves fail me, d'you know what I mean? I mean it was me nerves that failed me the last time, to be honest with you, because you know the way they take you out in threes, Tone, right? I started off behind this bloke – he was a Chinese bloke actually. Now: my bloke had told me to turn left, right? Now, we came to the first Give Way, and the bloke in front slammed his brakes on. Now, I'm going behind him, and I suppose I'm going a little bit too quick with me nerves; so I slam on my brakes, and I went slap in the back of him.

ANGELA: Ah.

BEVERLY: Now, I reckon that prejudiced my examiner against me.

ANGELA: What a shame.

BEVERLY: Yeah, it was, actually. Can you drive, Ang?

ANGELA: No. I'd like to learn, but Tony won't let me. He doesn't think I'd be any good. And it's a shame, 'cos it's so awkward for me to get to work since we've moved.

BEVERLY: Is it, yeah?

ANGELA: And you see, I could use the car when he wasn't working.

BEVERLY: And that would make you completely independent of Tone, wouldn't it?

    [Pause.]

D'you pass your test first time, Tone?

TONY: Yeah.

BEVERLY: I thought so, actually – he looks the type, doesn't he? [She goes to the bar.] Who's for another drink? Ang?

ANGELA: Thanks.

BEVERLY: How about you, Tone?

TONY: Ta.

BEVERLY: Yeah? Great.

    [Enter Laurence.]

BEVERLY: What's the matter?

LAURENCE: Nothing. Tony, I wonder if you could give me a hand for a moment, please?

BEVERLY: Won't the car start?

LAURENCE: No.

ANGELA: Go on, Tony!

TONY: All right!

    [Tony follows Laurence out.]

BEVERLY: Mind you don't go getting dirt on your suit. All right, Tone? [She concludes pouring drinks.] Ang.

ANGELA: Thanks.

BEVERLY: Cheers.

ANGELA: Cheers.

BEVERLY: Ang: would you mind if I asked you a personal question?

ANGELA: No.

BEVERLY: Now, please don't be offended when I say this, but, what colour lipstick are you wearing?

ANGELA: A pinky red.

BEVERLY: A pinky red! Now, can you take a little bit of criticism? Please don't be offended when I say this, but, you're wearing a very pretty dress, if I may say so; now, you see that pink ribbon down the front? If you'd chosen, Ang, a colour slightly nearer that pink, I think it would have blended more with your skin tones; d'you know what I mean?

ANGELA: A paler colour.

BEVERLY: A slightly paler colour. Now, can I give you a tip?

ANGELA: ... yes.

BEVERLY: Now, okay. I can see what you've done: you've just sat down in front of your mirror, and you've put your lipstick on. Now, this is something I always used to tell my customers, and it always works ... now, next time, just sit down in front of your mirror, and relax. And just say to yourself, 'I've got very beautiful lips.' Then take your lipstick and apply it, and you'll see the difference, Ang. Because then you will be applying your lipstick to every single corner of your mouth, d'you know what I mean? Will you try it for me next time?

ANGELA: Yes.

BEVERLY: Just sit down in front of your mirror, and relax, and say to yourself –

ANGELA: 'I've got very beautiful lips.'

BEVERLY: And I promise you you'll see the difference, Ang! Okay?

ANGELA: Thanks.

[*The front door bell chimes.*]

BEVERLY: Would you excuse me just one minute, Ang?

[*Beverly goes out. Angela helps herself to a cheese-pineapple savoury. Meanwhile, starting offstage:*]

BEVERLY: Hi, Sue.

SUSAN: Hello, Beverly.

BEVERLY: Come in.

SUSAN: Thank you.

BEVERLY: All right, Sue?

SUSAN: Yes, thank you.

BEVERLY: Come through.

SUSAN: I'm sorry I'm a bit late.

BEVERLY: Now, don't worry, Sue, that's all right. Would you like to slip your jacket off?

SUSAN: Oh, thank you.

BEVERLY: Everything all right, Sue?

SUSAN: Yes, I think so. I hope so.

BEVERLY: Come through and say hello. Ang: this is Sue. Sue, this is Ang.

ANGELA: Hello.

SUSAN: How d'you do.

BEVERLY: Sue's from Number 9.

ANGELA: Oh, we've just moved into Number 16.

SUSAN: Oh, really?

BEVERLY: Yeah, you know the Macdonalds' old house, Sue?

SUSAN: Yes.

BEVERLY: Yeah. Sit down, Sue. I'll just pop your coat in the hall. [*Going*] Won't be a sec. Make yourself at home, Sue!

SUSAN: Thank you. [*She puts a wrapped bottle on the bar, and proceeds to sit down.*]

ANGELA: We've only been here a fortnight.

SUSAN: Oh, really?

[*Beverly returns.*]

BEVERLY: Did you bring that, Sue?

SUSAN: Yes.

BEVERLY: Is it for us?

SUSAN: Yes.

BEVERLY: Oh, thank you, Sue!

SUSAN: It's nothing very special, I'm afraid.

BEVERLY: Ah. Isn't that kind, Ang?

ANGELA: Yes.

SUSAN: Not at all.

BEVERLY [*Unwrapping the bottle*]: Oh, lovely! 'Cos Laurence likes a drop of wine, actually. Oh, it's Beaujolais. Fantastic! Won't be a sec, I'll just pop it in the fridge. [*She goes to kitchen.*]

ANGELA: I'm so pleased to meet you. I want to meet all the neighbours.

SUSAN: Yes.

[*Beverly returns.*]

BEVERLY: Now, Sue: what would you like to drink?

SUSAN: I'll have a glass of sherry, please.

BEVERLY: Sherry, are you sure?

SUSAN: Yes. Thank you.

BEVERLY: 'Cos we've got everything. There's gin, whisky, vodka, brandy, whatever you'd like. Would you like a little gin-and-tonic, Sue? 'Cos me and Ang are drinking gin-and-tonic, actually.

SUSAN: All right – thank you.

BEVERLY: Ice and lemon?

SUSAN: Yes, please.

BEVERLY: Great.

ANGELA: It's a nice drink, gin-and-tonic, isn't it?

SUSAN: Yes, it is.

ANGELA: Refreshing. [*Tony returns during:*] Sometimes I drink lager-and-lime. Say I'm in a pub with my husband, I'll drink that. But I prefer this.

TONY: Can I wash me hands, please?

BEVERLY: Yes, just one second, Tone, while I finish making Sue's drink. Sorry: Sue – this is Tony.

ANGELA: My husband.

SUSAN
TONY }: How d'you do.

ANGELA: Did you push it all right?

TONY: Yeah. The battery was flat.

BEVERLY: Sue!

SUSAN: Thank you.

BEVERLY: Cheers.

SUSAN: Oh, cheers.

BEVERLY: Now. Tony, hands! Come through. (*She takes him to kitchen.*] Soap and towel there. Okay?

TONY: Ta.

ANGELA: D'you work?

SUSAN: No. No, I don't.

ANGELA: I'm a nurse.

SUSAN: Oh.

ANGELA: At St Mary's in Walthamstow.

SUSAN: Oh, yes.

ANGELA: Beverly says your daughter's having a party. Is that right?

SUSAN: That's right, yes.

ANGELA: Has it started yet?

SUSAN: Yes. Yes, it has.

BEVERLY: All right, Tone?

TONY: Yes, thank you.

BEVERLY: Come through.

    [*He comes through.*]

Drink's on there. Like to sit down?

TONY: Ta.

BEVERLY: Now then, Sue, let's see ... would you like a little cigarette?

SUSAN: Oh. No, thank you.

BEVERLY: Are you sure?

SUSAN: Yes. Thank you.

BEVERLY: Perhaps you'll have one a little bit later on. And I know Angela doesn't want one. Now, everybody all right?

TONY: Yes, thank you.

ANGELA: Yes, lovely, thanks.

SUSAN: Yes. Thank you.

BEVERLY: Yes? Great!

[*Rock music starts at Number 9, not especially loud.*]

BEVERLY: Aye aye! It's started, Sue.

ANGELA: They've got the record-player going, haven't they? They're going to have fun, aren't they?

BEVERLY: Sounds like it.

SUSAN: I hope so.

ANGELA: How old is she, your daughter?

SUSAN: Fifteen.

ANGELA: What does she look like? 'Cos I might have seen her.

SUSAN: Oh. Well, she's quite tall, and she's got fair hair, quite long fair hair.

ANGELA: She hasn't got a pink streak in her hair, has she?

SUSAN: Yes.

BEVERLY: Yeah, that's Abigail! And she wears those jeans, Ang, with patches on, and safety-pins right down the side, and scruffy bottoms.

ANGELA: Yes, I've seen her.

SUSAN: And plumber's overalls.

BEVERLY: Yeah, plumber's overalls. She makes me die, you know!

ANGELA: I've seen her: she was standing outside your gate with a friend. And you've seen her as well, haven't you? Getting off that motorbike.

TONY: Yeah.

ANGELA: How many people are coming to the party?

BEVERLY: About fifteen, isn't it, Sue?

SUSAN: Well, it was fifteen. Then it went up to twenty, and last night I gathered it was twenty-five.

BEVERLY: It's creeping up, Sue.

SUSAN: I've told her that's the limit. Well, I think that's enough. Don't you?

BEVERLY: Definitely, Sue, yeah, definitely.

ANGELA: Yeah.

BEVERLY: But, this is it with teenagers: okay, they tell you twenty-five; but a friend invites a friend: that friend invites another friend;

and it creeps up till you end up with about seventy or eighty. This is it. This is the danger!

TONY: I've just seen a couple of people arriving, actually.

SUSAN: Yes. Nice of them to help you with the car.

TONY: Oh, no – not them: a couple of coloured chaps and a girl roared up in a Ford Capri.

SUSAN: Oh, really? [*Pause.*] Well, there were only half a dozen there when I left ... When I was asked to leave.

BEVERLY: Yeah, this is it, isn't it? They don't want Mum sitting there, casting a beady eye on all the goings-on, do they?

ANGELA: No. Not when they get to fifteen. When I was fifteen I really wanted a party of my own, and my Dad, he'd never let me. You see, I've got four sisters. Haven't I, Tony?

TONY: Yeah.

ANGELA: And I think he was a little bit worried that I'd invite all my friends, and they'd bring along a few of theirs, and we'd end up with a houseful.

BEVERLY: This is it.

ANGELA: And he was worried about people pinching things, and things getting broken.

BEVERLY: Have you locked your silver away, Sue?

SUSAN: No, I haven't got any. Well, not much, anyway. I've put a few things upstairs; just in case of accidents.

ANGELA: Yes, well, it's better to, isn't it? 'Cos it can easily happen.

BEVERLY: Yeah.

ANGELA: Like that egg-timer. Tony was furious. It was a wedding present.

BEVERLY: Don't get me wrong, Sue: I wasn't meaning that any of Abigail's friends are thieves – please don't think that. But, you don't know who you get at a party. And let's face it: people are light-fingered.

ANGELA: Yes.

[*Pause.*]

BEVERLY: D'you leave your carpets down, Sue?

SUSAN: Er – yes.

ANGELA: Have you got fitted carpets?

SUSAN: Yes.

ANGELA: Yes ... we've got fitted carpets. The Macdonalds left them all. They were inclusive in the price of the house.

SUSAN: Oh?

ANGELA: And we're very lucky, because we got the price of the house down from twenty-two thousand to twenty-one thousand.

SUSAN: Really?

ANGELA: I don't know what we'll do about our carpets when we have a party. 'Cos we're having a party soon, aren't we?

TONY: Housewarming.

ANGELA: Yeah. You'll have to come.

SUSAN: Thank you.

BEVERLY: This is it, though, isn't it, with fitted carpets you don't know what to do for the best. Particularly with teenagers. Because let's face it, they're not as careful as, say, we would be, d'you know what I mean, they don't think; I mean, they've got a drink in one hand, a cigarette in the other, they're having a bit of a dance, and the next thing you know is it's cigarette on your carpet, and stubbed out.

ANGELA: Is it your daughter's birthday?

SUSAN: No. She just wanted a party. No particular reason.

BEVERLY: Yeah, well, they don't need a reason these days, do they? Any excuse for a bit of a rave-up – what do they call it, freak out? D'you get that beer, Sue?

SUSAN: Yes. I got four of those big tins, and some Pomagne.

ANGELA: Oh, that's nice, isn't it?

SUSAN: Yes, it is.

BEVERLY: It's funny, at that age we used to drink Bulmer's Cider. We used to say, 'A glass of cider, and she's anybody's.'

ANGELA: I got very drunk on champagne at our wedding. D'you remember?

TONY: Yeah.

BEVERLY: Gives you a terrible headache, champagne, doesn't it?

ANGELA: Yes. In the morning.

BEVERLY: Yeah, shocking. D'you get any spirits, Sue?

SUSAN: No. No, I didn't.

BEVERLY: No. You're very wise. 'Cos they're so expensive, aren't they? And let's face it, if they want to drink spirits, they can bring their own. Particularly the older boys. 'Cos they're working, aren't they? I mean, there will be older boys at the party, won't there?

SUSAN: Oh, yes.

BEVERLY: Yeah. Well, let's face it, Ang, when you're fifteen you don't want to go out with a bloke who's fifteen, do you?

ANGELA: No.

BEVERLY: 'Cos they're babies, aren't they? I mean, when I was fifteen, I was going out with a bloke who was twenty-one.

[Pause.]

How's Abigail getting on with that bloke, by the way, Sue?

SUSAN: I'm not sure: I daren't ask.

BEVERLY: Mind you, I reckon you're better to let her go out with as many blokes as she wants to at that age, rather than sticking to the one. Don't you agree with me, Ang?

ANGELA: Yes. How many boyfriends has she got?

SUSAN: I don't know. I don't think she really knows herself.

ANGELA: Footloose and fancy free!

BEVERLY: Actually, Sue, I was just thinking: it might be a good idea if a little bit later on, if Laurence and Tony pop down there. Now I don't mean go in; but, just to check that everything's all right; put your mind at rest. Don't you agree with me, Ang?

ANGELA: Yes, it's a good idea. You don't mind do you?

TONY: No.

SUSAN: It's very nice of you. But I don't think it'll be necessary.

TONY: Your husband's away, then, is he?

SUSAN: No. We've split up, actually.

ANGELA: Are you separated, or divorced?

SUSAN: Divorced.

ANGELA: When did you get divorced?

SUSAN: Three years ago.

ANGELA: Oh, well: that's given you time to sort of get used to it, hasn't it? We've been married three years – three years in September, isn't it?

BEVERLY: Yeah, me and Laurence have been married three years, actually.

ANGELA: Oh, it's funny – we were all getting married about the same time as you were getting divorced!

SUSAN: What a coincidence.

ANGELA: Yes! Where is he now? D'you know?

SUSAN: Yes. He lives quite near here, actually.

ANGELA: Oh, that's nice. D'you keep in touch?

SUSAN: Yes.

BEVERLY: Yeah, he pops over to see the kids, doesn't he, Sue?

SUSAN: Yes. He comes every Sunday.

ANGELA: Does he?

SUSAN: For lunch.

ANGELA: Ah, lovely. Is he coming tomorrow?

SUSAN: I expect so.

ANGELA: Ah, that's nice – for the kids.

BEVERLY: Yeah, well, let's face it, Sue, whatever you say about him, he is their father, isn't he?

SUSAN: Yes.

BEVERLY: Mind you, I don't believe in people sticking together for the sake of the kids. To me, that is wrong. I mean, take my parents, for example. Now, you might not believe this, Sue, but it's the truth: my parents have not spoken to each other for twenty years, and as long as I can remember, my father has slept in the box-room on his own.

ANGELA: Yeah, well, that's like my father: he's terrible to my mother.

BEVERLY: Is he?

ANGELA: He hardly speaks to her.

BEVERLY: Yeah. You see, it's not fair, is it, Ang? I mean, take my mum, right? She's sixty and she's ever so sweet – she wouldn't hurt a fly. But, she's really ill with her nerves. And why? It's a result of all the rows that have been going on.

ANGELA: Yes, well, that's like my mum. She's been very ill for five years, seriously ill with a blood disease.

BEVERLY: Ah!

ANGELA: She might die at any moment.

BEVERLY: Really?

ANGELA: But it doesn't make any difference: my dad's still as rotten to her as he's always been.

BEVERLY: Is he? Yeah, you see, it's not fair, is it! I mean, this is the truth: if my father was to drop dead tomorrow, I wouldn't care. 'Cos I hate him. We all hate him. But, he's the kind of bloke, he'll live till he's ninety. Whereas your Mum, bless her, she could do with her good health, and she hasn't got it. Now to me, it's all wrong. I mean, they say The Good Die Young, and I'm afraid it's true.

ANGELA: Yeah, well, it's like Tony's dad: he just walked out and left Tony's mum, and you were only about three, weren't you?

TONY: You like living round here, do you?

SUSAN: Yes. It's a very pleasant area.

  [Pause.]

ANGELA: What did your husband do?

SUSAN: He's an architect.

ANGELA: Oh, that's a good job, isn't it?

SUSAN   ⎱ Yes, it is.
BEVERLY ⎰ · Yeah, it's a good job, architect.

ANGELA: Well paid.

SUSAN: Yes, it can be. It's quite a long training, though.

ANGELA: Yes.

BEVERLY: Has David married again, Sue?

SUSAN: Yes.

ANGELA: Oh, well: it's a good job that he's got a good job, then, isn't it? I mean, if he's got two families to support.

BEVERLY: Have they got any children, Sue?

SUSAN: No. But she wants some. So they're trying. But they don't seem to have had any success so far.

ANGELA: Does she come over on Sundays?

SUSAN: No, he comes on his own.

ANGELA: Oh, but I suppose like, when your kids go over there, it's nice for her 'cos she's got a little ready-made family.

SUSAN: Well, they don't go over there, actually. Well, hardly ever.

ANGELA: Don't you get on with her?

SUSAN: No. Well – I hardly know her, really.

ANGELA: Well, I mean . . . if your husband runs off with another woman, well . . . !

BEVERLY [going to bar]: Well, let's face it, Ang, you can hardly be the best of mates, can you, d'you know what I mean?

ANGELA: No.

BEVERLY: Now, would anybody like another drink? Ang?

ANGELA: Thanks.

BEVERLY: Sue?

SUSAN: I still have some, thank you.

BEVERLY: Yeah, come on, Sue: I'll just give you a little top-up. That's it. Now, Tone: another drink?

TONY: Ta.

[Beverly pouring drinks.]

ANGELA: I think more and more people are getting divorced these days, though.

BEVERLY: Yeah, definitely, Ang. Mind you, I blame a lot of it on Women's Lib. I do. And on permissiveness, and all this wife-swapping business. Don't you, Tone?

TONY: I suppose so.

BEVERLY: Don't you, Sue?

SUSAN: Possibly.

BEVERLY: I mean, take Peter Sellers for example. Now he had been married at least five or six times.

SUSAN: Four, actually.

BEVERLY: Is it four, Sue?

ANGELA: Well, look at Elizabeth Taylor and Richard Burton.

BEVERLY: Now to me, their relationship was ridiculous. I think they made a mockery of marriage. I think it was disgusting.

ANGELA: They only did it for the publicity.

BEVERLY: I mean, with these film stars, I reckon half the time the attraction is purely physical.

ANGELA: They did it in the jungle.

BEVERLY: Yeah. I mean, to a film star, getting divorced is like going to the lavatory, if you'll pardon my French. But to us, it's a big wrench, isn't it, Sue?

SUSAN: Yes, of course.

ANGELA: Yes.

SUSAN: But I think that film stars only get married because the public expects it.

BEVERLY: Do you?

SUSAN: Yes. I do.

ANGELA: I think people take divorce for granted. I think if they stuck it out, they'd be all right, don't you?

BEVERLY: Yeah. But, mind you, there are times, Ang, let's face it, when you could hit them on the head with a rolling-pin, and clear out. D'you know what I mean?

ANGELA: Yeah, well, that's like Tony and me. I mean we've only been married nearly three years, but we're always having rows, aren't we?

TONY: Yeah.

BEVERLY: She give you a bad time, Tone?

TONY [taking a drink]: Ta. Shocking.

ANGELA: And I think it spoils things, doesn't it?

SUSAN: Yes, it does.

BEVERLY: Mind you, I reckon a little row sometimes adds a sparkle to a relationship. You know.

ANGELA: Did you have a lot of rows with your husband?

SUSAN: No, we didn't, actually.

ANGELA: Oh.

BEVERLY: Well, there you go, you see, it doesn't always follow. It's funny, isn't it? D'you think people should get married, Tone?

TONY: Sometimes.

ANGELA: Oh, he's not so sure, you see, since he's been married to me!

BEVERLY: Perhaps we should all live in sin, and forget the whole, thing, I don't know.

ANGELA: Did you live with Laurence before you got married?

BEVERLY: No, I didn't, actually.

ANGELA: D'you think if you had have done, you'd still have married him?

BEVERLY: No, I don't honestly think I would have done. Don't get me wrong: I do love Laurence, in my own way. But, if we'd have lived together, say for a year, I don't honestly think it would have worked out.

[*Pause.*]

TONY: I think if you're going to have kids you ought to get married.

BEVERLY: Oh, yeah, definitely, Tone, give them a name, yeah.

ANGELA: Yes.

BEVERLY: You'll be having all this soon, Sue. Do you think Abigail is the marrying type?

SUSAN: I hope so.

ANGELA: Oh, you'll probably be getting married again yourself soon!

SUSAN: Oh, I don't think that's very likely.

ANGELA: You never know. 'Cos I never thought anyone would marry me. And you see, I met Tony and we were married within a year, weren't we?

TONY: Eight months.

ANGELA: Yes. So you see, it can happen.

SUSAN: Really?

ANGELA: Have you got a boyfriend?

SUSAN: No.

[*Pause.*]

BEVERLY: Would you like to have kids, Ang?

ANGELA: Yes. Yes, I would.

BEVERLY: Would you, Tone?

TONY: Not for a while.

ANGELA: Not till we get settled in.

BEVERLY: Yeah, get yourself sorted first, yeah. He'd make a nice dad, though, wouldn't he?

ANGELA: Yes.

BEVERLY: I could just see you, actually, with a little boy – you know: taking him out, and looking after him!

ANGELA: Be nice to have one of each.

BEVERLY: Yes, like Sue. It's funny, though, with Sue's kids, to me, Abigail and Jeremy aren't a bit alike. Are they, Sue?

SUSAN: No. They're not.

BEVERLY: They're like chalk and cheese, Ang.

ANGELA: Do they take after you or your husband?

SUSAN: Neither of us, really: Jeremy looks more like my brother. Abigail doesn't look like anyone in the family.

BEVERLY: The Black Sheep. Eh, Sue: how did Jeremy get on packing his little overnight bag?

SUSAN: Oh, he loved it!

BEVERLY: Did he? Yeah! You know what kids are like, Sue was telling me, he was so excited about packing all his little things.

SUSAN: He'd have taken the kitchen sink, if I'd let him.

ANGELA: Where's he gone?

SUSAN: Round the corner.

TONY: How old is he?

SUSAN: Eleven-and-a-half.

[Pause.]

ANGELA: Would you like kids?

BEVERLY: No, I don't think I would, actually. Don't get me wrong, it's not that I don't like kids, 'cos I do, but, let me put it to you this way: I wouldn't like to actually have to have them. I mean – did you have your kids in hospital, Sue?

SUSAN: Yes.

ANGELA: Did you have an easy labour?

SUSAN: Well ... Abigail was really very difficult. But Jeremy was fine. He was born very quickly.

BEVERLY: Yes, you see, to me, having to go into hospital would be like being ill, and I couldn't stand that. And I know it sounds horrible, but all that breast-feeding, and having to change nappies, would make me heave. I don't honestly think I've got that motherly instinct in me.

ANGELA: You see, it'd be different for me, 'cos I'm used to looking after children.

BEVERLY: Yeah.

ANGELA: And if I can look after a wardful of sick children, I can easily manage a couple of my own.

BEVERLY: Yeah.

ANGELA: Because the thing is, with children that are ill, is, that you've got to watch them every minute. Like, recently, we had this little girl, she was only about two, and she kept picking at her dressing. She picked it all off, and got right down into the wound –

BEVERLY: I'm sorry, Ang, but would you stop? It's just that if you carry on, I'll faint.

TONY: Leave it out, Ang!

ANGELA: No, it's all right, 'cos she wasn't in any pain, but she actually got the stitches –

TONY: Drop it!!

[Pause.]

ANGELA: Did you know my husband used to be a professional footballer?
BEVERLY: Really?
ANGELA: Yes, he used to play for Crystal Palace, didn't you?
TONY: Yeah.
BEVERLY: Oh, that is fantastic.
ANGELA: That was before I met him.
BEVERLY: What, d'you used to play for the reserves, Tone?
ANGELA: Oh, no; it was the first team.
BEVERLY: Honestly, is that true?
TONY: Yeah:
BEVERLY: You're not kidding me?
ANGELA: No.
BEVERLY: What, honestly, the first team?
TONY: For a bit, yeah.
BEVERLY: Oh, that is fantastic. Hey, Sue, we didn't know we had a celebrity moved into Richmond Road, did we?
SUSAN: No, we didn't.
BEVERLY: That is fantastic, Tone: that's really made my night, actually.
    [*Enter Laurence. He stops, registers suddenly remembering something, curses silently, spins round, and rushes out.*]
BEVERLY: Laurence! [*She gets up.*] Would you excuse me a minute? [*Going*] Laurence!
    [*Exit Beverly. Pause. We can still hear Abigail's music.*]
ANGELA: Nice music. Isn't it, Tony?
    [*Pause. Tony gets up and picks up a plate of cheese-pineapple savouries.*]
TONY: Would you like one of these?
SUSAN: Thank you.
    [*Angela gestures for one. He gives her one silently.*]
ANGELA: Ta. I shouldn't be eating these. 'Cos we had a big tea. Did you eat earlier?
SUSAN: Er ... no. No, I didn't!
ANGELA: Oh, you must be hungry. Here, have some peanuts.
SUSAN [*taking some*]: Thank you.
ANGELA: Are they having a barbecue?
SUSAN: No.
ANGELA: Oh, 'cos it's a nice idea, that, if you've got a big garden.
SUSAN: Yes, it is.
ANGELA: I'd love to have a barbecue – you know, do baked jacket potatoes ...
SUSAN: Lovely ...

ANGELA: Have sausages and chops. And you can do chestnuts. And have an ox – you know, on a spit!

[*Enter Beverly.*]

BEVERLY: Hey, it's all happening at your place, Sue. Oh, it's so funny, Ang. You know your bay window, Sue, at the front? – Well, it's wide open and there's this bloke, Ang, he's gotta be twenty stone and he's wedged in your bay window; he's got one of those purple vests on, you know? – and a great big fat belly. And there's a girl, Sue, standing in your front garden, she's as thin as he's fat, and she's draped round him like this, Ang, and they're snogging away – you've never seen anything so funny in all your life!

SUSAN: Oh, dear.

BEVERLY: Now – don't worry, Sue: 'cos they're only having a bit of fun, I mean, they're only teenagers, aren't they?

SUSAN: I wonder if I dare just pop down there for a minute.

TONY: Would you like me to go and have a look for you now?

SUSAN: Er, no.

ANGELA ⎫ . Tony doesn't mind.
TONY ⎭ ˙ It's no problem.

SUSAN: No . . . ; thank you; but I think perhaps it's better not.

BEVERLY: No, Sue's right: it's best not to pop down there. They're only having a bit of fun. And let's face it, when Laurence gets back we can discuss it then. Okay? Now, who's for another drink? Come on, Ang!

[*Angela joins Beverly at the bar.*]

How about you, Sue?

SUSAN: No, thank you.

BEVERLY: Yeah, come on, Sue, give you a little top-up, just to settle your nerves. That's it. How about you, Tone? Another drink?

TONY: Ta. Where is Laurence, anyway?

BEVERLY: I don't know, actually, Tony. I wish I did know.

[*Angela is wandering round the room.*]

ANGELA: Oh, what a lovely table. This is just what we need. It's the next thing we're going to get. 'Cos at the moment we're eating off our knees. It's unusual, isn't it? – with the wooden top and the modern legs.

BEVERLY: Yeah; it was expensive, that one, actually.

ANGELA: Yes. Ah! – and this is what I'd really love!

BEVERLY: What, the candelabra? Yeah, it's brilliant, isn't it?

ANGELA: Yes. Is it real silver?

BEVERLY: Yeah, silver plate, yeah.

ANGELA: Yes. And it looks so lovely, and with the light.

[*Angela wanders into the kitchen. Beverly gives Susan her drink.*]

BEVERLY: Sue.

SUE: Thank you.

BEVERLY: You all right, Sue?

SUSAN: Yes, fine, thank you.

BEVERLY: Yeah. [*Pause.*] Sue, you must think I'm dreadful! I do apologize: I haven't offered you anything to eat. I'm sorry! Have some nuts.

SUSAN: Thank you.

BEVERLY: Take some crisps, as well.

SUSAN: Thank you.

BEVERLY: Now then, Sue, let's see ... would you like a little cheesy-pineapple one?

SUSAN: Thank you.

BEVERLY: Tone? A little cheesy-pineapple one?

TONY: Ta.

BEVERLY: Take another one, Sue – save me coming back.

SUSAN: Thank you.

BEVERLY: Now then, Sue – a little cigarette?

SUSAN: No, thank you, not just at the moment.

BEVERLY: Sorry, Sue – I'll tell you what I'll do: I'll pop it on here for you, Sue, and then you can light it when you've finished those. Okay? Lovely.

ANGELA [*from kitchen*]: Tony, come and have a look at this beautiful kitchen!

BEVERLY: It's lovely, isn't it?

ANGELA: Oh, these tiles are gorgeous. Were they here when you came?

BEVERLY: Yeah, we were lucky, actually.

ANGELA: You were. 'Cos our kitchen's nothing like this. Tony, come and have a look.

BEVERLY: Yeah, go and have a look, Tone, they're beautiful, actually; go on – go and have a look.

ANGELA: Tony!

BEVERLY: Go on.

[*Tony goes.*]

ANGELA: Is this a freezer part with your fridge?

BEVERLY: Yes, it's a freezer at the top, yeah. [*To Sue*] He's nice, isn't he?

SUSAN: Yes.

BEVERLY: Yeah, he's fantastic. Yeah ... they're a very nice couple, actually; aren't they?

SUSAN: Yes.

ANGELA: Oh, the sink's got its own light.

TONY: Leave it!

ANGELA: And you've got one of these!

BEVERLY: What, the rotisserie? Yeah.

ANGELA: D'you cook chickens and things on it?

BEVERLY [joining Angela and Tony]: Well, you can do, but to be honest I'm not much of a cook, so I haven't actually used it yet, but you can do. And you can also do kebabs, they're very nice.

ANGELA: Oh, lovely.

[Laurence has entered, with a carrier bag.]

BEVERLY: Would you excuse me, Tony?

LAURENCE: Oh, hullo, Sue. You all right?

SUSAN: Yes, fine, thank you.

BEVERLY: Laurence, where have you been, please?

LAURENCE: To the off-licence.

BEVERLY: Those want to go in the fridge, Laurence, to chill. Sorry, Ang, sorry, Tone – come through!

ANGELA: Thanks.

BEVERLY: Like to sit down?

TONY: Ta.

[Laurence has taken the lagers to the kitchen. Angela and Tony sit down.]

BEVERLY: Now then, Sue, let's see ... that little cigarette ...

SUSAN: Oh, thank you.

BEVERLY [lighting Sue's cigarette]: There we are, Sue.

SUSAN: Thank you.

BEVERLY: Now; everybody all right?

ANGELA ⎫ Yes, thanks.
TONY   ⎬ : Yes, thank you.
SUSAN ⎭ Yes ... thank you.

BEVERLY: Great.

[Beverly collects her drink and sits. Laurence returns from the kitchen. Pause.]

LAURENCE: Right now: who's for a drink? Tony, light ale?

TONY: Not just yet, thank you.

BEVERLY: Go on; Tone, have a light ale, 'cos he got them specially for you.

LAURENCE: If he doesn't want one, he doesn't have to have one, Beverly. Sue?

SUSAN: No, thank you.

LAURENCE: Angela?

ANGELA: No, I'm all right, thanks.

LAURENCE: Beverly?

BEVERLY: No, I'm fine, thank you.

LAURENCE: Laurence? Yes, please. [*He gets his glass.*] Thanks very much.
    [*Only Angela laughs. Laurence pours his drink.*]

LAURENCE: Well, the party certainly seems to be hotting up at your
    place, Sue.

SUSAN: Yes ... so Beverly said.

BEVERLY: Yeah, we were just saying, actually, Laurence, it might be a
    good idea if a little bit later on, if you and Tony would pop down
    there.

LAURENCE: What for?

BEVERLY: Just to check that everything's all right, for Sue – put Sue's
    mind at rest. Because I know she's a little bit worried.

SUSAN: I think it'll be all right.

LAURENCE: Yes, Sue, I don't think there'll be any problems.

SUSAN: No.

BEVERLY: Laurence, I'm not saying there'll be any problems – all I'm
    saying is, would you please pop down for Sue?

ANGELA: You don't mind, do you, Tony?

BEVERLY: No, of course he doesn't mind.

TONY: No, I don't mind.

LAURENCE: Well, I've just been past, and everything seems to be all
    right.

ANGELA: Didn't you see what was happening in the garden?

LAURENCE: Well – yes ...

ANGELA: The couple, snogging through the window?

LAURENCE: Through the window?

ANGELA: With the dirty vest?

LAURENCE: No. No, I saw a couple down the side of the house, and
    there were a few in the porch. But I didn't see anybody in the window.

TONY: Would you like to sit down here, Laurence?

LAURENCE: No, no – you stay where you are.

ANGELA: No, sit here – there's plenty of room.

LAURENCE: Thank you.

    [*Laurence sits on the sofa between Angela and Susan.*]

LAURENCE: Anyway, Sue: these sort of things, they happen at parties.

SUSAN: Yes, of course.

LAURENCE: I'm sure it's nothing to worry about.

SUSAN: No.

BEVERLY: Actually, Laurence, I think you're being very unfair to Sue.

SUSAN: Oh, not at all.

BEVERLY: Now, Sue, don't make excuses for him. And apart from anything else, Tony has already agreed to go actually.

LAURENCE: Oh, have you?

TONY: Yeah.

LAURENCE: Yes, well, I didn't say I wouldn't go. If she wants us to go down there, surely, of course we'll go.

SUSAN: Well, I don't know that I do, really.

LAURENCE: Fine.

ANGELA: Tony doesn't mind going on his own, do you?

TONY: No, I don't.

LAURENCE: I didn't say I wouldn't go.

BEVERLY: Fine, then, Laurence, are you going, please?

LAURENCE: Yes.

BEVERLY: Thank you.

LAURENCE: That's quite all right.

　　[*Pause.*]

BEVERLY: I'm not saying there'll be any trouble, but, with teenagers, they have a drink, and they get over-excited –

ANGELA: Yes, well, it starts with one kiss ...

BEVERLY: –then they find their way to the bedrooms.

　　[*Pause.*

　　Sue flicks ash from her cigarette.]

LAURENCE: Sue: do you like olives?

SUSAN: Yes.

LAURENCE [*getting up*]: Fine: I'll get you some!

SUSAN: Thank you.

　　[*Laurence goes to the kitchen.*]

BEVERLY: You've got a friend for life there, Sue.

SUSAN: Oh?

BEVERLY: None of us like olives, you see.

SUSAN: Ah, I see.

BEVERLY: I can't stand them. It's those stuffed olives – you know that little red bit that sticks out? Well, it reminds me of – well, I'm not going to say what it reminds me of, but I can't eat them, it puts me off.

　　[*Laurence has returned.*]

LAURENCE: Sue?

SUSAN: Thank you.

[*During following Laurence sits between Susan and Angela, and eats a couple of olives. After a while he starts looking for something in his pockets.*]

ANGELA: Well, not everyone can like everything, can they? It's like Tony, he doesn't like curry, and I love it. So we never go in Indian Restaurants now, do we?

TONY: No.

ANGELA: And you can get English food in Indian Restaurants – I mean you can have chips with your meal instead of rice. But you see Tony had a bad experience in an Indian Restaurant – this was before I knew him –

BEVERLY: Yes?

ANGELA: He had a nasty dose of gastro-enteritis after he'd had a curry, and you see that put him off.

BEVERLY: Yes.

ANGELA: And he won't even eat curry at home, now. Which is a shame, because I enjoy making it; it's a good way of using up leftovers. Have you ever tried pilchard curry?

BEVERLY: No.

ANGELA: That's a very economical dish. And it's easy: just get one of those big tins of pilchards in tomato sauce, and mix it with curry powder and onions, and it's really tasty.

BEVERLY: Oh?

ANGELA: I used to share this flat with these girls, and we often used to do that. But you see, Tony won't touch it. But then, I don't like Turkish Delight, and you see, Tony loves that.

[*Laurence is looking in his pockets for something.*]

BEVERLY: Darling, have you got heartburn?

LAURENCE: No.

BEVERLY: Have you got heartburn?

LAURENCE: No, I haven't got heartburn. [*Laurence gets up and goes to his case.*] Just a slight case of indigestion, that's all.

[*During following, Laurence gets out an antacid tablet and eats it. Then he gets out a small cigar.*]

BEVERLY: I thought so. This is it, you see, Ang. He came in late, and he was all upset; 'cos he's very highly strung, Sue, and this gives him heartburn.

ANGELA: He must be careful, then; because when I was working in intensive care, the people who'd had a cardiac arrest, they were nearly all business men, and those who were worrying about their work.

BEVERLY: I hope you're listening to this, Laurence.

LAURENCE: Yes, I'm listening! Cigar?

TONY: No, thank you. I've just given up.

LAURENCE: Are you sure?

BEVERLY: Yeah, go on, Tone, take a little cigar, enjoy yourself, go on, take one!

LAURENCE: Yes, go on, take one.

TONY: Thank you. [*He takes one.*]

ANGELA: Tony! Oh, well, that counts, doesn't it? I mean, if he's having a cigar ...

BEVERLY: Yeah, come on, Ang!
   [*Angela taking a cigarette.*]

LAURENCE: Sue –

ANGELA: Thanks!

LAURENCE: Would you like one?

SUSAN: Er – no, thank you.

LAURENCE: Some women do like them, you know, Sue?

SUSAN: Yes, so I understand, but I've got a cigarette.

LAURENCE: Oh. [*To Tony*] Light?

TONY: Ta.

ANGELA: 'Course, smoking's one of the chief causes of heart disease.

SUSAN: But it's just contributory, isn't it?

ANGELA: Well, yes, but if somebody's got a tendency towards that condition, they really shouldn't smoke.

LAURENCE: No, no, no. I don't believe that smoking, in moderation, can do any harm at all.

BEVERLY: Laurence, would you like to put a record on for us, please?

LAURENCE: Yes, surely; what would you like to hear?

BEVERLY: Feliciano.

LAURENCE: Oh, no, Beverly. [*Going to records*] We don't want to listen to that blind Spaniard caterwauling all night.

BEVERLY: Darling, not classical.

LAURENCE: Light classical – just as background. [*Producing a record*] Sue, d'you know James Galway?

SUSAN: Yes, I've heard him.

LAURENCE: He's a very up-and-coming young flautist. Do you like him?

SUSAN: Yes, he's very good.

LAURENCE: Fine, I'll put it on for you.

BEVERLY: Laurence, I'm sorry, but we don't want to listen to classical music at the present moment.

LAURENCE: Well, what do you want to listen to, then, Beverly?

BEVERLY: Feliciano.

LAURENCE: Well, if everybody wants to listen to Feliciano, we'll put it on.

BEVERLY: Tone, d'you like Feliciano?

TONY: Yeah, I do.

BEVERLY: Yeah, he's fantastic, isn't he? Sue?

SUSAN: I don't know him, I'm afraid.

ANGELA: Oh, you'll like him. He's lovely.

BEVERLY: Yeah, Sue, he's really great. Sue: would you like to hear him?

SUSAN: Yes ...

BEVERLY: Yeah? Laurence, Angela likes Feliciano. Tony likes Feliciano, I like Feliciano, and Sue would like to hear Feliciano: so please: d'you think we could have Feliciano on?

LAURENCE: Yes.

BEVERLY: Thank you.

  [*During following, Laurence puts on the record (José Feliciano:* Feliciano, *Track One,* California Dreamin').]

ANGELA: Oh, it changes colour, doesn't it?

BEVERLY: What, the fibre-light? Yeah! Isn't it beautiful, Ang?

ANGELA: Oh, it's lovely!

BEVERLY: Yeah ... D'you know what I do, Ang? I put a record on, and I sit in that chair, and I just gaze at it for hours.

ANGELA: Do you?

BEVERLY: Yeah. It's funny, it always reminds me of America. I don't know why, but it does.

  [*Pause.*]

ANGELA: Oh, yes, it's New York, isn't it?

BEVERLY: Yes, I suppose it is, really ...

ANGELA: How are you enjoying your cigar?

TONY: Very nice, thank you: how's your cigarette?

ANGELA: Oh, it's lovely. Mind you don't choke on it! You see, he's not used to smoking a cigar: he doesn't know what to do with it.

BEVERLY: He'll be all right. Tone: would you like another drink?

TONY: Ta.

BEVERLY: Yeah? How about you, Ang?

ANGELA: Please.

BEVERLY [*taking glass*]: Thanks. Sue?

SUSAN: Oh, no, thank you.

BEVERLY [*taking Sue's glass*]: Yeah, come on, Sue – I'll give you a little top-up. That's it.

[*Beverly is joined at the bar by Tony. The music is just starting. During following, Laurence returns to sit between Angela and Susan.*]

BEVERLY: Like to help yourself, Tone?

TONY: Ta.

BEVERLY: It's a fantastic drink, Bacardi, isn't it?

TONY: Yeah.

BEVERLY: Yeah.

TONY: I first started drinking it when I went to Majorca.

BEVERLY: You've been to Majorca?

TONY: Yeah.

BEVERLY: Ah, great. Where d'you go?

TONY: Palma.

BEVERLY: Not Palma Nova?

TONY: That's right, yeah?

BEVERLY: Oh, fantastic – isn't it beautiful there?

TONY: Yeah.

BEVERLY: They drink it very long there, don't they, with lots of ice and Coke and all that, yeah. It's my dream, actually, just lying on the beach, sipping Bacardi-and-Coke.

ANGELA: Have you always had a moustache?

LAURENCE: What d'you mean?

ANGELA: Have you had it for a few years?

SUSAN [*given drink*]: Thank you.

LAURENCE: Yes.

ANGELA: Never thought of having a beard to go with it?

LAURENCE: No.

BEVERLY: No, Laurence wouldn't suit a beard, Ang, his face is too small.

LAURENCE: Actually, I think a beard can look very scruffy.

ANGELA: Yes, but I think a man with a moustache and a beard, they look more masculine.

BEVERLY: Sexier, isn't it?

ANGELA: Mmm. Has your husband got a beard?

SUSAN: No, no. He used to have ... a long time ago ... when I first knew him.

ANGELA: Why did he shave it off?

SUSAN: Well, he grew out of it.

[*Pause.*]

LAURENCE: Do you play any instruments yourself, Sue?

SUSAN: No. No, I used to play the piano when I was a child.

LAURENCE: Oh, the piano?

SUSAN: Just a little.

LAURENCE: I once went for guitar lessons ... but I never kept them up.

SUSAN: That's a pity.

LAURENCE: Yes, I've often regretted it.

  [*Pause.*]

LAURENCE: You know, I think musicians and artists, they're very lucky people: they're born with one great advantage in life. And d'you know what that is? Their talent. They've got something to cling to. [*Pause.*] I often wish I'd been born with that sort of talent. [*Pause.*] Most people, they just drift through life, without any real aims. They're weak. It's no good just sitting there, whining. You've got to get up, and do something about it. Not that it isn't a fight. Of course it is. Life is a fight – people always seem to be against you. Not that I've done badly – oh, no: I've done all right! But it's certainly an uphill battle.

ANGELA: I once went to a party, and they said, 'Can anyone play the piano?' And I said, 'Oh, yes, I can.' And you see, I can't play the piano – I'd just learned this one tune from a friend. It was

> 'Buy a broom
> Buy a broom
> Buy a broom,

> And sweep the room!'

– And that's all I knew. And you see, they wanted me to play for musical chairs. So I started:

> 'Buy a broom
> Buy a broom ...'

– And I played it a few times.

BEVERLY: Yeah?

ANGELA: And then I thought, well, I'll have to do something a little bit different. So I started, y'know, just –

BEVERLY: What, vamping?

ANGELA: Yeah.

BEVERLY: Yes.

ANGELA: But as I can't play, it sounded terrible. And I felt such a fool. I thought, why did I say, y'know, I'd play?

BEVERLY: When was this, Ang?

ANGELA: Oh, it was only when I was eight.

BEVERLY: Oh, I see!

ANGELA: Oh, yes. I still felt a fool, though.

BEVERLY: Would anybody mind if I turned this next track up? Because it's my favourite, it's 'Light My Fire', and I'd like us all to hear it. Anybody mind?

ANGELA
TONY   : No.
SUSAN

BEVERLY: No? Great. [*She turns record up.*] Fantastic, isn't he?

ANGELA: Yeah. I know this one.

BEVERLY: Yeah? D'you think he's sexy, Ang?

ANGELA: Yes. But it's a pity he's blind.

BEVERLY: Yeah. Mind you, I reckon that makes him more sensitive. D'you know what I mean?

ANGELA: Mmm. Yes.

  [*Beverly proceeds to dance solo in front of the others, and across the room.*]

BEVERLY: D'you like him, Tone?

TONY: Yeah.

BEVERLY: Knockout, isn't he?

  [*Beverly continues dancing, helping herself to a crisp as she passes by the coffee-table.*]

BEVERLY: This used to turn me on at parties, Tone, eight years ago – that's how long I've liked him. [*More dancing.*] And, imagine making love to this? D'you know what I mean?

  [*Angela laughs.*]

BEVERLY [*squeezing Laurence's shoulder*]: Are you all right, Laurence?

  [*Beverly dances away from the others with her back to them. Laurence suddenly jumps up, rushes to the stereo and turns it off.*]

LAURENCE: Are you ready, Tony?

BEVERLY: Thank you, Laurence!

LAURENCE: Don't mention it. Are you ready?

TONY: What for?

LAURENCE: Well, Sue wants us to go and inspect the party; I think we should go and inspect it.

BEVERLY: Fine, Laurence: would you like to go now, please?

LAURENCE I am going.
SUSAN   Oh, but, I really think it would be better –

BEVERLY: It's all right, Sue.

LAURENCE: Are you coming, Tony?

TONY: I think so.

LAURENCE: Well, come on, then!

  [*Laurence goes. Tony gets up to follow ...*]

SUSAN: I really think it would be better if you didn't.

TONY: It's all right. Just take a walk past your house: put your mind at rest.

BEVERLY: Don't worry, Sue; Tony'll handle it.

TONY: Won't be long.

BEVERLY: Take care.

[*Exit Tony. Pause.*]

BEVERLY: I'm sorry about that.

ANGELA: Oh, that's all right. Shall I put the record on again?

BEVERLY: No, don't bother, Ang, because he's spoiled it now.

ANGELA: Oh, and you were enjoying yourself!

BEVERLY: Yeah, well we were all enjoying ourselves, weren't we? [*Pause.*] To be quite honest, he's a boring little bugger at times, actually. [*Pause.*] Anyway, sod him. Come on, let's all have a drink!

ANGELA: Yeah.

BEVERLY: Come on , Sue!

SUSAN: Oh, no, really –

BEVERLY [*taking Susan's glass*]: Yeah, come on, Sue, that's it!

[*Angela has joined Beverly at the bar.*]

BEVERLY: I'll tell you what: let's all get pissed. Yeah!

ANGELA: Yeah. We can enjoy ourselves.

BEVERLY: Yeah. Cheers, Ang!

ANGELA: Cheers!

BEVERLY: Cheers, Sue.

SUSAN: Thank you.

ANGELA: Cheers!

SUSAN: Cheers.

BEVERLY: Come on, Ang: have a little cigarette while he's gone, sod him.

ANGELA: Oh, yeah, while he's out.

BEVERLY: Yeah, come on. That's it.

[*Beverly and Angela light their cigarettes.*]

SUSAN: I think I'm going to be sick.

ANGELA: Are you? Come along, then.

BEVERLY: Come on, Sue.

ANGELA: Where's the toilet?

[*Angela and Susan are on the way out of the room.*]

BEVERLY: Under the stairs, Ang, in the hall. Take deep breaths, Sue.

ANGELA: Hold on a minute.

BEVERLY: Take deep breaths: you'll be all right.

[*Pause. The following from offstage . . .*]

ANGELA: That's the way. Bring it all up. That's it. Better out than in.
    [*Beverly reacts.*]

BLACKOUT

ACT II

Same as Act I. A bit later. Beverly has put the lights on, and is pouring drinks.
Enter Angela.

ANGELA: She'll be all right now.

BEVERLY: Yeah, she'll be all right, Ang.

ANGELA: I've just left her on her own for a minute, to sort herself out.

BEVERLY: Yes. She's been sick, hasn't she?

ANGELA: Yes.

BEVERLY: Yeah. And I'm making her a little black coffee, Ang, so that'll help to revive her a little bit, you know?

ANGELA: Mmm.

BEVERLY: Cheers, Ang.

ANGELA: Cheers!

BEVERLY: Cheers!

[*They drink. We can still hear Abigail's music.*]

ANGELA: I think she's had a few too many gin-and-tonics.

BEVERLY: So do I.

ANGELA: And on an empty stomach.

BEVERLY: Really?

ANGELA: Oh, yes – she's not had anything to eat tonight.

BEVERLY: Now, she's silly, isn't she? She should have had a meal.

ANGELA: Yeah, well, we had a big meal earlier on.

BEVERLY: Yeah, well, I had a meal.

ANGELA: We had lamb chops.

BEVERLY: Did you? Yeah, I had a little frozen pizza.

ANGELA: And she's trying to keep up with us.

BEVERLY: Yeah, yeah; and another thing, Ang, I think she's the type, her nerves, give her a nervous stomach. She has a few drinks, and that makes her sick.

ANGELA: I knew that, and I thought, that's what brought this on.

BEVERLY: Yeah. And it's a shame, 'cos she's ever so nice, isn't she?

ANGELA: Yes.

BEVERLY: Yeah.

ANGELA: I feel a little bit sorry for her.

BEVERLY: So do I, Ang.

[*Enter Susan.*]

ANGELA: All right?

SUSAN: Er – yes ... thank you.

BEVERLY: All right, Sue? – ah, come through. That's it. She still looks a little bit pale, doesn't she, Ang?

ANGELA: Yes. [*Taking Susan's glass*] I'll take that.

SUSAN: Thank you. Sorry.

BEVERLY: Don't worry, Sue. That's all right.

ANGELA: Come and sit down. That's it. You sit down here and your soda-water's there. Now, lean forward a minute, lean forward.

[*She props an extra cushion behind Susan's back.*]

That's it. Lovely. All right.

BEVERLY [*coming from kitchen*]: Now look, Sue, I've made you a little black coffee, now I've made it nice and strong, and I haven't put any milk in it, case that makes you sick again. All right?

SUSAN: Actually, I think it would be better if I didn't.

BEVERLY: Are you sure, Sue?

SUSAN: Yes.

BEVERLY: Oh, all right, then, I'll tell you what I'll do: I'll pop it on here for you. Now, will you try and sip that for me, Sue? – because it will help to revive you. All right?

ANGELA: Have you got a headache?

SUSAN: Yes, just a bit.

BEVERLY: Would you like a little Aspro, Sue?

SUSAN: Oh, no, thank you.

BEVERLY: Are you sure?

SUSAN: Yes.

ANGELA: No, she's better just with soda-water, 'cos she'll only bring it up.

BEVERLY: I've got it! Just a minute; let's see ... [*looking in her handbag*] yeah, here we are. Now look, Sue, this is only a very light perfume ...

SUSAN: I'm all right, actually!

BEVERLY [*applying perfume to Susan's face*]: Now, Sue, it will just help to freshen you up a little bit. Because when you've been vomiting, Ang, you feel horrible, don't you?

ANGELA: Yeah.

BEVERLY: Yes. That's it. [*Applying some to her own hand*] It's lovely, actually. It's Estée Lauder, 'Youth Dew'.

ANGELA: Mmm.

BEVERLY: Would you like to try some, Ang?

ANGELA: Oh, yes!

BEVERLY: Yeah.

[*Angela helps herself to a liberal dose.*]

BEVERLY: You only need a little drop, Ang!

ANGELA: Oh.

BEVERLY: 'Cos it's quite strong, actually, yeah. That's it.

ANGELA: Mmm, it's nice.

BEVERLY: Yes, it's beautiful, isn't it? Now does that feel a little bit fresher, Sue?

SUSAN: . . . Thank you.

BEVERLY: Yeah?

[Pause.]

SUSAN: Sorry about that.

ANEGLA: Oh, there's no need to be sorry, is there?

BEVERLY: Sue – Don't worry. Let's face it, it could happen to any of us, couldn't it?

ANGELA: Yes, and it's better for it to happen while those two are away.

BEVERLY: Definitely, yeah.

SUSAN: I wonder – could you pass me my handbag, please?

ANGELA: Yes, where is it?

SUSAN: It's, um, on the floor.

[While Angela gets the handbag, Susan removes the cushion from behind her.]

ANGELA: Here we are.

SUSAN: Thank you.

BEVERLY: No, 'cos when you're vomiting in front of blokes, Ang, it's embarrassing, isn't it?

ANGELA: Yes. And they're not usually that sympathetic.

BEVERLY: No.

ANGELA: Well, I know Tony isn't. 'Cos if I've got a headache, or my period pains, he doesn't want to know.

BEVERLY: Really?

ANGELA: In fact, it annoys him.

BEVERLY: Now, this is it, you see; I reckon a woman, she needs a bit of love and affection from a bloke. Okay, sex is important. But, Ang, it's not everything.

ANGELA: No. You see, if Tony comes home, and he's in a bad mood, I can't do anything right. 'Cos they pick on you, don't they?

BEVERLY: Is he like that?

ANGELA: Oh, yes, he's very quick-tempered.

BEVERLY: Is he?

ANGELA: I think it's because of his red hair.

BEVERLY: Yeah. It's funny, isn't it, Sue? To see him, sitting there, he looks ever so quiet and gentle, doesn't he?

SUSAN: Yes.

BEVERLY: Is he very violent?

ANGELA: No, he's not violent. He's just a bit nasty. Like, the other day, he said to me, he'd like to sellotape my mouth. And that's not very nice, is it?

BEVERLY: It certainly isn't, Ang!

ANGELA: Was your husband violent?

SUSAN: No, not at all. He was a bit irritable sometimes, a little difficult. But – I think we all are.

ANGELA: Ah! She's one of the lucky ones, isn't she?

BEVERLY: Definitely, Sue, definitely.

ANGELA: Mind you, if Tony wasn't around, I'd miss him.

BEVERLY: Would you?

ANGELA: Yes.

BEVERLY: Yeah. It's funny, isn't it? I suppose I would miss Laurence inasmuch as I need a bloke – well, let's face it, we all need a bloke, don't we? And, okay, credit where it's due: he's very good with money. I mean, if I want a new dress, make-up, have my hair done, whatever it is, the money is there. But, apart from that, it's just boring, know what I mean?

ANGELA: Yes. Well, I think that comes from being married, doesn't it?

BEVERLY: Do you?

ANGELA: The fun wears off.

BEVERLY: Yeah.

ANGELA: Oh, your cushion's slipped.

SUSAN: I'm all right, actually.

ANGELA: Come on, lean forward.

BEVERLY: Yeah, come on, Sue.

ANGELA: Make you comfy.

BEVERLY: 'Cos Angela knows.

  [Enter Laurence.]

ANGELA: Everything all right down there?

LAURENCE: Yes, I think so.

BEVERLY: How many's at the party, then?

LAURENCE: Well, I don't know – I didn't stop to count them. [To himself] This is my glass. [He goes to the bar.]

SUSAN: It's all right, is it?

LAURENCE: Yes!! – Oh, I'm sorry, Sue: Yes, yes, I went in, and I had a few words with them, and everything seems to be all right.

ANGELA: Where's Tony got to?

LAURENCE: Perhaps you'd better ask him that, when he gets back.

SUSAN: Did you see Abigail?

LAURENCE: I certainly did.

SUSAN: Is she all right?

LAURENCE: I think so.

ANGELA: Where is he?

LAURENCE: I don't know. I'm not his keeper.

SUSAN: Did you talk to her?

LAURENCE: Well, I asked her to turn the music down, yes.

ANGELA [to Beverly]: He's stayed at the party!

SUSAN: Was she upset?

LAURENCE: I don't think so.

BEVERLY [to Angela]: He's probably being raped by a load of fifteen-year-old schoolgirls!

ANGELA: Oh, lucky them!

BEVERLY: I'll tell you something: at least they had a bit of taste – they didn't pick him! [Indicating Laurence.]

ANGELA: I hope he's feeling a bit more enthusiastic than when I leap on him!

BEVERLY: Is he one of those?

ANGELA: Yes, he turns over.

BEVERLY: I've met those before, actually.

LAURENCE [going to case for antacid tablet]: Beverly!

BEVERLY: Ang, I can just see it, right, the music's thumping away, and your Tone's lying on the floor, and there's all these girls, right, you know, piling on top of him, and your Tone just turns over, and goes to sleep.

LAURENCE: That's enough, Beverly!!

BEVERLY: Oh, Christ, Laurence! Every time I'm enjoying myself . . . !

LAURENCE: Can't you see you're embarrassing Sue?

BEVERLY: Oh, now I'm sorry, Sue. Now, listen, I didn't mean to embarrass you, Sue; it was only a little joke; all right?

ANGELA: You see, Sue's not been feeling too good, anyway.

BEVERLY: No.

LAURENCE: Oh, really? What's been the problem, Sue?

SUSAN ⎫. Oh, it was nothing.
BEVERLY ⎭ She's been vomiting, actually.

LAURENCE: That's all right, thank you, Beverly! Sue can speak for herself!

ANGELA: You see, she's had a few too many gin-and-tonics, and you've not had any tea, have you?

SUSAN: No.

BEVERLY: No.

LAURENCE [*offering her a cheese-pineapple savoury*]: Well, would you like one of these, Sue?

SUSAN: Er, no, thank you.

BEVERLY: Laurence, she doesn't want one of those on an empty stomach, now does she?

LAURENCE: A sandwich, then. Would you like a sandwich, Sue?

SUSAN: No, thank you.

BEVERLY: Laurence, she doesn't want a sandwich!

LAURENCE: Well, I want a sandwich! Now do you want a sandwich, Sue, yes or no?!

SUSAN: No. Thank you.

LAURENCE: Okay. Fine!

[*Laurence rushes to the kitchen, and starts to make a sandwich.*]

BEVERLY: I hope it chokes you!

[*Laurence rushes back from the kitchen, with a kitchen-knife in one hand, and a tub of margarine in the other.*]

LAURENCE [*pointing the knife at Beverly*]: What did you say, Beverly?

BEVERLY [*shrieking*]: Oh, Christ, Ang, I'm going to get stabbed.

LAURENCE: Don't tempt me.

BEVERLY: Well, go on, then: do it!

[*Pause. Then Beverly pushes away the knife.*]

BEVERLY: Laurence, would you please go back in the kitchen and finish making your little sandwich, all right?

[*Pause.*]

LAURENCE: Are you sure you don't want a sandwich, Sue?

SUSAN: Yes. Thank you.

LAURENCE: Fine.

[*Laurence goes back to the kitchen. Pause. Then the front door bell chimes. Angela and Beverly shriek with renewed mirth.*]

ANGELA: Oh, he's here at last. They must've let him out!

BEVERLY: They've obviously had their fill!

[*The following from offstage:*]

TONY: Everything all right?

LAURENCE: What d'you mean?

TONY: I wondered where you'd got to.

LAURENCE: Yes, well, I wondered where you'd got to. Come in.

TONY: What's that for?

LAURENCE: I'm making a sandwich! Go in.

[*Laurence returns to kitchen. Enter Tony. He looks slightly flushed and dishevelled.*]

ANGELA: Where've you been?

TONY: Southend.

ANGELA: Did you enjoy yourself there?

TONY: Wonderful!

ANGELA: Where've you been? – Laurence has been back for ages.

TONY [to Susan]: Everything's all right – nothing to worry about!

SUSAN: Good. Not too rowdy?

TONY: No.

SUSAN: Thank you.

TONY: 't's all right.

　　　[Beverly has joined Tony near the bar.]

BEVERLY: Would you like a drink?

TONY: Yes, please.

BEVERLY: What would you like?

TONY: Light ale, please.

BEVERLY: Like a little Bacardi to go with it?

TONY: No, thank you.

BEVERLY: Are you sure?

TONY: Yeah.

BEVERLY: Are you all right?

TONY: Yeah.

BEVERLY: Great!

　　　[She fixes the drink, whilst:]

SUSAN: Was Abigail all right?

TONY: I think so.

SUSAN: You saw her?

TONY: I didn't actually see her, but I think she's all right.

BEVERLY [giving drink]: Tone.

TONY: Ta.

BEVERLY: Your shirt's all wet.

ANGELA: What is it?

TONY: Nothing.

BEVERLY [feeling his chest]: But you're soaking wet!

ANGELA [getting up]: What've you been doing?

TONY: Nothing.

　　　[Angela feels his chest.]

Get off! [To Susan] I just bumped into somebody accidentally – minor incident: nothing to worry about.

BEVERLY: D'you want to sit down, Tone?

TONY: Ta.

ANGELA: Laurence didn't come back with his shirt all wet, did he?

BEVERLY: Dead right he didn't. Laurence comes back looking like he's
   spent a day at the office.

ANGELA: I don't think you two have been to the same party, have you?

TONY: 'Course we've been to the same party. What are you talking
   about?

BEVERLY: Ah, lay off her, Tone – she's only having a little joke.

ANGELA: See what I mean?

TONY: What?

   [*Susan gets up.*]

BEVERLY: Are you all right, Sue?

SUSAN: Yes. But I think I'd better go and see Abigail myself.

BEVERLY: No, Sue, please. Don't go down there. Now, listen to me,
   Sue: you know what Abigail is like, now, she's only going to
   shout at you, and then you'll be upset. Now please, Sue, come
   on, sit down. Now look, Tony's only just come back – now, it was
   all right, wasn't it, Tone?

TONY: Oh, yeah.

BEVERLY: Yeah?

TONY: There's nothing to worry about.

SUSAN: Are you sure?

TONY: Yep.

BEVERLY: Yeah – now come on, Sue, sit down. Now I'll tell you
   what I'll do, I'll put a little record on for us, ey? Yeah! Then we can all
   have a little listen to that, yeah. Now, let's see what we've got ...
   Tell you what now, look, Sue: d'you like Elvis?

SUSAN: Yes, he's all right.

BEVERLY: Yeah, he was great, wasn't 'ee? D'you like him, Ang?

ANGELA: Mmm.

BEVERLY: Yeah. Now we'll put this on for Sue ...

   [*Beverly puts on the record (Elvis Presley:* Elvis's 40 greatest, *Track
   One,* Don't). *Whilst she is doing so:*]

ANGELA: Is Abigail always having parties?

SUSAN: No.

   [*Pause.*]

BEVERLY: Ready, Ang?

ANGELA: Mmm.

   [*The music starts.*]

BEVERLY: Oh, isn't he great?

ANGELA: Yeah!

BEVERLY: Yeah. [*Pause.*] I won't be a sec, I'm just going to the toilet,
   all right?

[*Exit Beverly.*
Laurence, having finished making his sandwich, has been sitting with it for some time at the dining table. As she passes him on her way, Beverly gives him a squeeze.
Long pause.
Laurence gets up, adjusts his dress, and goes to the stereo. He turns down the volume.]

LAURENCE: That's better. Now at least we can hear ourselves think.

ANGELA: D'you want to sit here.

LAURENCE: No, thank you.

ANGELA: Come on ...

LAURENCE: No, thanks!!

TONY: Steady!

[*Pause.*]

LAURENCE: I expect you've seen a few changes since you've been here, eh, Sue?

SUSAN: Not really, no.

ANGELA: When did you move here?

SUSAN: In 1968.

ANGELA: Oh, you've been here a long time, then, haven't you?

SUSAN: Yes.

ANGELA: D'you think you'll stay here?

SUSAN: Till the children are older.

ANGELA: Oh, yes, then I suppose when you're on your own, you'll get somewhere a little bit smaller?

SUSAN: Yes, I expect so.

LAURENCE: Oh, come on, Sue – surely you must have seen some changes?

SUSAN: Well ... there are the new houses on the other side of Ravensway.

LAURENCE: Ah, yes, the houses! But what about the people?

SUSAN: What about them?

LAURENCE: The class of people, now don't you think that's changed.

SUSAN: Not really, no.

LAURENCE: The tone of the area – don't you feel it's altered?

SUSAN: Not particularly.

LAURENCE: You don't think it's gone down?

SUSAN: No.

[*Pause.*]

LAURENCE: And you, Tony, yes, come on, what do you think, eh?

TONY: I wouldn't know, would I?

LAURENCE: Oh, no – of course! You've only just moved in yourselves, haven't you?

ANGELA: Yes.

TONY: Yes.

LAURENCE: Yes! Drink?

TONY: No, thank you.

LAURENCE: Angela?

ANGELA: Please.

[*Laurence takes Angela's glass, and proceeds to fix her drink.*]

SUSAN: It's more mixed, that's all.

LAURENCE: Mixed? Yes, I suppose you could say it was mixed! – More cosmopolitan.

SUSAN: There's nothing wrong with that.

LAURENCE: Oh, you don't think there's anything wrong with that?

SUSAN: No, I don't.

LAURENCE: Well, that's a matter of opinion. Would you like another drink, Sue?

SUSAN: I'm just drinking soda-water, thank you.

LAURENCE: Fine: would you like some more soda-water?

SUSAN: Thank you.

LAURENCE [*getting Susan's glass*]: We like to keep our guests happy. [*Fixing Susan's drink*] Do you read, Tony?

TONY: Sometimes.

LAURENCE [*giving drink*]: Sue.

SUSAN: Thank you.

LAURENCE: Have you read any Dickens?

ANGELA: Oh, yes. I've read *David Copperfield*.

LAURENCE: *David Copperfield*? Well, I have the Complete Works here. [*He takes one book out, and displays it.*]

ANGELA: Oh, they're a lovely set, aren't they?

LAURENCE [*demonstrating book*]: Yes, they are very well-bound. They're embossed in gold.

ANGELA: Mmm ... really nice.

[*Laurence displays it briefly to Tony; then goes over to Sue for a demonstration.*]

LAURENCE: Sue

SUSAN: Very nice.

[*He shows her the pages, then offers it to her.*]

LAURENCE: Please!

SUSAN [*taking book*]: Thank you!

LAURENCE: And just what do you read, eh, Tony?

TONY: All sorts.

LAURENCE: All sorts! – well, for instance?

ANGELA: What was that one you were reading?

TONY: *Computer Crime*.

LAURENCE: *Computer Crime*!! – ooh, that sounds interesting. D'you know Shakespeare?

TONY: Not personally. I read it at school, yeah.

LAURENCE: Oh, at school!

> [*Laurence has gone to his set of Shakespeares.*
> *Enter Beverly and sits down.*
> *Laurence takes out one volume, demonstrates it, then selects a page.*]

Macbeth. [*Pause.*] Part of our heritage. [*Pause; he puts it back.*] Of course, it's not something you can actually read. Sue?

SUSAN [*returning Dickens*]: Thank you.

> [*Laurence replaces Dickens.*]

ANGELA: Your house is a lot older than ours, isn't it?

SUSAN: Yes.

LAURENCE: Sue: 1936. Yes?

SUSAN: I'm not sure. But it was built before the war.

LAURENCE: I thought so.

ANGELA: Oh, there's nothing wrong with an old house. I mean, there's some quite nice ones. I like old and I like new. I like those old Tudor houses round here.

LAURENCE: No, Angela: Mock-Tudor.

ANGELA: Are they?

LAURENCE: Oh, yes. There are some real Tudor properties in Hadley Village itself. But the ones you're thinking of are Mock-Tudor.

ANGELA: The trouble with old houses is they haven't got any central heating.

LAURENCE: Ah, yes, but of course central heating can be installed into older properties. It may cause some shrinkage of the beams, etcetera, but, if it's done by an expert, there shouldn't be any problems. D'you know the Belvedere Hotel?

ANGELA: Yes. Yes, I do.

LAURENCE: Yes, well, originally, on that site stood a Tudor mansion.

ANGELA: Oh, it doesn't look very old.

LAURENCE: No, no, the present property is late Victorian – neo-Gothic. No, no, the original building, the mansion house, was Tudor. They owned all the land round here.

BEVERLY: D'you want another, Ang?

LAURENCE: I've seen to the drinks, thank you, Beverly!

[*The following dialogue runs simultaneously with the preceding passage, and starts after Laurence's line 'It may cause some shrinkage of the beams'.*]

BEVERLY: You all right, Sue?

SUSAN: Yes, thank you.

BEVERLY: You don't feel sick again, do you?

SUSAN: No.

BEVERLY: No.

SUSAN: No. It seems to be settling.

BEVERLY: Good. You all right, Tone?

TONY: Yes, thank you.

BEVERLY: Great.

[*Beverly gets up and goes over to Tony.*]

D'you want a drink?

TONY: Ta.

BEVERLY: D'you want another, Ang?

LAURENCE: I've seen to the drinks, thank you, Beverly!

BEVERLY: Oh, I'm sorry, Laurence: it's just that I can't hear through two brick walls.

[*Beverly goes to the bar.*]

LAURENCE: Yes, er . . . it was all part of the Belvedere Estate.

BEVERLY: Laurence, would you like to turn that record up, please?

LAURENCE: How can we hold a conversation with that racket blaring out?

BEVERLY: Laurence, we're not here to hold conversations, we are here to enjoy ourselves. And for your information, that racket happens to be the King of Rock'n'Roll.

LAURENCE: Oh, really? Well, I always thought that Bill Haley was the King of Rock'n'Roll!

[*Beverly turns the volume up. Laurence turns it off. Beverly goes to turn it on; Laurence grabs her arm. Pause: they are locked together.*]

BEVERLY: All right, Laurence.

[*Pause. He lets go. Pause.*]

LAURENCE: Sorry about that.

ANGELA: Oh, that's all right. We're all getting a little bit merry, aren't we? And it's nice for us to have a chance to enjoy ourselves, 'cos since the move, we've hardly been out.

[*Susan gets up.*]

BEVERLY: Where are you going, Sue?!

SUSAN: Er . . . I'm just going to the toilet.

BEVERLY: You don't feel sick again, do you?

SUSAN: No, I'm fine, thank you.

ANGELA: D'you want me to come with you?

SUSAN [*going*]: No, thank you.

[*Exit Susan.*]

BEVERLY: Give us your glass, Ang. I'll give you a little top-up.

ANGELA: You see, Sue's been vomiting up her gin, and while you were away, I had to take her to the lavatory.

BEVERLY [*giving drink*]: Ang.

ANGELA: Thanks.

BEVERLY: Cheers, everyone. Cheers!

ANGELA: Cheers!

LAURENCE: Cheers!

TONY [*miming his glass*]: Cheers!

BEVERLY: Oh, I'm sorry, Tone, I forgot your light ale, didn't I? I do apologize.

LAURENCE: I'll get it.

BEVERLY: Thank you, Laurence! [*Beverly sits. Pause.*] Ang: shall we have a little dance?

ANGELA: Yeah. Be nice.

BEVERLY: Tone: d'you fancy a little dance?

TONY: Yeah, I don't mind.

BEVERLY: Yeah?

LAURENCE: There's no room to dance in here, Beverly.

BEVERLY: Laurence, if I'd wanted somebody to put a damper on the idea, I would have asked you first, okay? Come on, Ang: give us a hand moving the couch. Come on.

[*Laurence gives Tony his drink.*]

TONY: Ta.

[*Beverly and Angela prepare to move the couch.*]

BEVERLY: Got it?

TONY ⎫ It's all right, Beverly, I'll do that.
LAURENCE ⎭ : I'll do it, Angela.

[*The men take over.*]

ANGELA: I'll take this end.

LAURENCE: No, you just sit down.

BEVERLY: Cheers, Tone.

TONY: You got it, Laurence?

LAURENCE: Yes.

[*Tony and Laurence pick it up. Laurence drops his end.*]

BEVERLY: Oh, for Christ's sake, Laurence!

LAURENCE: Don't interfere, Beverly. You ready?

TONY: Where d'you want to put it?

LAURENCE [*to Beverly*]: Well, where d'you want it?

BEVERLY: Oh, for God's sake: just put it back there!

LAURENCE: Just back.

[*Tony and Laurence move the couch.*]

BEVERLY: Ang, I've got this fantastic record I'm gonna play for us, right? Just hang on a sec. Now, this record, Ang, it turns my husband on, and when he hears it, he cannot resist my charms.

[*Beverly proceeds to put on the record (Sam-The Man-Taylor & His Orchestra, or any similar 'smoochy' music). During this:*]

ANGELA: They're still enjoying themselves down there, aren't they?

TONY: Yes.

ANGELA: What were they getting up to?

TONY: Nothing much.

BEVERLY: Ready, Ang?

ANGELA: Mmm.

[*The music starts.*]

BEVERLY: Fantastic, isn't it? Oh, I'm sorry, Laurence, is it too loud for you, my darling? I do apologize. I'll turn it down. Because we don't want to upset him, do we, Ang? (*She turns down the volume.*) Is that better? Fancy a little dance, Tone?

ANGELA: Dance with Beverly.

TONY: Perhaps Laurence'd like to dance?

BEVERLY: No, I don't think he would, actually. Come on, Tone: have a little dance, go on. [*Tony gets up and dances with Beverly. Angela and Laurence remain seated. After a short while, enter Susan.*] You all right, Sue?

SUSAN: Yes. Fine, thank you.

[*Susan sits. Pause. Beverly and Tony continue to dance.*]

BEVERLY: You don't mind me mauling your husband, do you, Ang?

ANGELA: No, you go ahead.

[*Pause.*]

TONY: Go on – dance with Laurence.

ANGELA: No, I can't.

TONY: 'Course you can: get up and dance!

BEVERLY: Don't worry, Ang – you'll be quite safe with Laurence. He won't rape you.

[*Angela gets up.*]

ANGELA: Would you like to dance?

LAURENCE [*getting up*]: Surely, if you'd like to.

[*Laurence places his glass on the coffee-table, and joins Angela; just as*

he reaches her, she starts 'bopping', which is inappropriate, as the music is 'smoochy', and Beverly and Tony are 'smooching'.
Laurence musters the vague gesture of a 'bop'.]

ANGELA [*whilst dancing*]: I'm not very good at these slow dances.

LAURENCE: No.

ANGELA: I'm better at this sort. [*Demonstrates a quick 'bop'.*] Would you like to dance with us?

SUSAN: Oh. No, thank you.

ANGELA: Come on – we can all three dance together!

SUSAN: No, really, I'm fine, thank you.

[*The dancing continues until the track ends.*]

LAURENCE [*shaking Angela's hand*]: Thank you.

ANGELA: Laurence was shaking my hand!

BEVERLY: Was he? Christ, he'll be shaking mine next. Now who'd like a drink? Ang?

ANGELA: Oh – please!

BEVERLY: Never say no! Tone, would you like a drink?

TONY: No, thanks, I'm all right.

BEVERLY: How about you, Sue?

SUSAN: No, thank you.

BEVERLY: Are you sure?

SUSAN: Yes.

BEVERLY: Yeah!

ANGELA: He's a good dancer, isn't he?

BEVERLY: He's fantastic.

ANGELA: I never knew you could dance so well. We don't usually dance like that, do we?

TONY: No.

BEVERLY [*giving drink*]: Ang!

ANGELA. Thanks.

BEVERLY: Cheers, everyone, cheers!

TONY
ANGELA } : Cheers!

SUSAN [*getting soda-water*]: Cheers.

BEVERLY: Darling, why don't you dance with Sue?

LAURENCE: I really don't think Sue wants to dance, thanks very much. Darling.

BEVERLY: Then why don't you ask her, Laurence?

[*Pause. Then Laurence gets up and crosses to Sue.*]

LAURENCE: Sue, would you like to dance?

SUSAN: Er, no, thank you.

LAURENCE: There you are – Sue doesn't want to dance!

BEVERLY: Of course she wants to dance! Go on, Sue, have a little dance with Laurence. Enjoy yourself, go on – have a little dance.

LAURENCE: Would you like to, Sue?

SUSAN: All right.

LAURENCE: I'll take your glass for you.

[*Laurence and Susan embrace formally. Beverly rejoins Tony.*]

BEVERLY: Come on, Tone.

[*Beverly and Tony go into a more intimate embrace than previously.*]

BEVERLY: Ang – d'you wanna dance with Tone?

ANGELA: No: you're all right.

[*Pause: the dancing continues.*]

LAURENCE: Are you going on holiday this year, Sue?

SUSAN: I hope so.

LAURENCE: Expensive business, holidays.

SUSAN: Yes.

LAURENCE: D'you know Paris?

SUSAN: A little.

LAURENCE: Oh. You've been there?

SUSAN: Yes. A long time ago. Have you?

LAURENCE: No. We're hoping to get there.

[*Pause.*]

SUSAN: I like Paris.

LAURENCE: Oh, yes ... Montmartre by night, the Champs Elysées, boulevard cafés ...

[*When the track ends, they stop dancing, Laurence shakes Susan's hand briskly and formally.*]

Thank you.

BEVERLY [*to Tony*]: Thanks very much.

TONY: Ta.

[*They all drift to seats except Tony. The empty seat is now between Susan and Beverly on the sofa.*]

BEVERLY: D'you wanna sit down, Tone?

TONY: Ta.

BEVERLY: Ang, do us a favour, throw us me fags. Would you, please?

[*Angela throws the cigarettes. Tony picks them up and gives them to Beverly.*]

Cheers, Tone. [*Tony leans back. The bar-flap now protrudes over the back of the sofa.*]

SUSAN: Mind your head.

ANGELA: It's too big.

TONY: What?

ANGELA: It's too big.

TONY: What is?

ANGELA: Your head.

TONY: Give it a rest!

[*Pause.*]

TONY: Feeling better now, are you?

SUSAN: Oh – much. Thank you.

TONY: Good.

[*Pause.*]

BEVERLY: Ang, d'you want a cigarette?

ANGELA: Oh, I would. Can I have a cigarette?

TONY: D'you want one?

ANGELA: I'd love one.

TONY: Why don't you have one, then?

[*Beverly throws a cigarette across to Angela. She lights it.*]

BEVERLY: Ang, do us a favour – give us a light, would you, please?

[*Angela goes over to light Beverly's cigarette. She returns.*]

ANGELA: You see, once you've had one cigarette, you want to keep on smoking, don't you?

BEVERLY: This is it, yeah.

SUSAN: What sort of work d'you do?

TONY: I'm in computers.

ANGELA: He's an operator.

BEVERLY: Still play football, Tone?

TONY } No –
ANGELA } No, he gave it up when he was twenty. He plays for the firm's team, though; and he's so much better than all the others.

TONY: It's not the firm's team, and I've only played twice!

ANGELA: He looks so funny in his shorts!

BEVERLY: Why d'you give it up?

TONY: Things didn't work out.

ANGELA: You've got footballer's legs, though, haven't you?

BEVERLY: Has he? Have you? Let's have a little look. Oh, yeah, so he has. I like footballer's legs, actually – they're nice and muscly, aren't they? Can't stand blokes with skinny legs, Ang, can you? Puts you off d'you know what I mean?

LAURENCE: Talking of Paris, Sue, do you like Art?

SUSAN: Er – yes.

LAURENCE: So do I. Beverly doesn't. Of course, Paris is the centre of the Art World. D'you like Van Gogh?

SUSAN: Yes.

LAURENCE [*crossing the room*]: This is a Van Gogh.

SUSAN: Yes.

LAURENCE: They called him a Post-Impressionist, but to my mind he was more of a symbolist. D'you like the Impressionists?

SUSAN: Yes.

LAURENCE: Oh, you do? That's good. Fine. Fine.

[*He crosses back to his seat. Sits.*]

BEVERLY: You all right, Tone?

TONY: Yeah!

BEVERLY: Great.

LAURENCE: Of course, you know, Van Gogh was a very unstable man. Not only did he cut his ear off and leave it in a brothel, he also ate paint, and he shot himself.

BEVERLY: Thank you, Laurence! We don't want all the gory details.

LAURENCE: I'm talking to Sue, and Sue is interested in these things.

[*He rushes across the room, and takes the Van Gogh off the wall.*]

LAURENCE: This is a picture of his chair in the corner of his room at Arles. It wasn't actually yellow, no, no, no: he painted it yellow because yellow symbolized so much for him.

BEVERLY [*turning record off*]: Shall we liven things up a bit?

TONY ⎫
ANGELA ⎭ : Yeah.

BEVERLY: Yeah?

LAURENCE: Do you like Art?

ANGELA: Yes!

LAURENCE: Good. This is a Lowry! Now, did you know, his father was an Estate Agent?

ANGELA: Oh.

BEVERLY: For Christ's sake, Laurence, give it a rest!

LAURENCE: Give what a rest?

BEVERLY: Nobody is interested.

LAURENCE: Oh, yes, they are!

BEVERLY: Oh, no, they're not!

LAURENCE: D'you know something, Beverly? You're ignorant?

BEVERLY: Oh, so I'm ignorant, now, am I?

LAURENCE: Now? You always have been!

BEVERLY: It's not a question of ignorance, Laurence, it's a question of taste!

LAURENCE: Taste! And what would you know about taste?

BEVERLY: The trouble with you, Laurence, is if somebody doesn't happen to like what you like, then you say that they've got no taste!

LAURENCE: That's rubbish!

BEVERLY: Oh, is it rubbish?

LAURENCE: Yes!

BEVERLY: Then what about that picture I've got upstairs in the bed-room, then?

LAURENCE: That is cheap, pornographic trash!

BEVERLY: Laurence, just because a picture happens to be erotic, it doesn't mean it's pornographic.

LAURENCE: Oh, shut up, Beverly!!

> [*Laurence rushes to the kitchen. During the following he is pouring and drinking a glass of water.*]

BEVERLY [*continuing immediately*]: I've got this fabulous picture, right, it's really beautiful; I brought it home, and he wouldn't let me put it up in here, oh, no: I had to hang it in the bedroom!

LAURENCE [*from kitchen*]: If I had my way it would be in the dustbin!

BEVERLY: Yeah, well, you're dead from the waist down anyway, let's face it!

ANGELA: Can I see it?

BEVERLY: D'you wanna see it, Ang?

ANGELA: Oh, yes.

TONY [*rising*]: Actually, Angela's got to be getting up early in the morning for work, so I think we ought to be going now.

SUSAN [*rising*]: Yes, I think I ought to be getting along ...

TONY: You can see the picture another time.

ANGELA: We don't have to go early just 'cos of me.

BEVERLY: You sure, Ang?

ANGELA: Yeah, I'll be all right!

LAURENCE [*having joined the others*]: She's got to get up in the morning!

BEVERLY: Oh, shut up, Laurence!

LAURENCE: Don't tell me to shut up!

TONY: Angela: COAT!!

ANGELA: No, it's all right.

SUSAN: I really think I ought to be going.

BEVERLY: Now don't be silly, Sue, because we haven't had a cup of coffee yet – now sit down.

> [*Exit Beverly.*]

LAURENCE [*following her*]: Beverly!

ANGELA [*to Susan*]: We're going soon, anyway.

> [*The following offstage:*]

LAURENCE: Beverly, don't bring that picture downstairs!

BEVERLY: Oh, sod off, Laurence!

LAURENCE: Beverly!

BEVERLY: Drop dead!!

TONY [*to Angela*]: You just can't keep your big mouth shut, can you?
GET UP!!

[*Angela gets up. Enter Laurence quickly. Goes to the stereo, looks for and finds a record, which he puts on the turntable. Then he turns on the machine. During the pause before the music actually starts:*]

LAURENCE: Sit down – please!

[*He sits. Angela sits. Susan sits. Tony does not sit. Laurence jumps up, goes to look at the record, walks towards the door, stops, looks at Tony, sits, waits. The music starts: Beethoven's* Fifth Symphony, *the first movement. Laurence now suffers a heart attack. He tries to suppress it for a time, as it approaches, whilst the others look on, confused. Then, a spasm, and he passes out. Angela, Susan and Tony go over to him during following.*]

ANGELA: Laurence? Laurence!

SUSAN: What's the matter?

TONY: What's wrong with him, Ang?

ANGELA: Just a minute.

[*Angela is examining Laurence: she loosens his tie.*]

TONY: Ang, what's wrong with him?

ANGELA: I don't know yet!

[*Angela examines Laurence's eyes.*]

Tony, can you help me get him on the floor? [*Angela and Tony move Laurence, helped by Susan. Enter Beverly, displaying picture* The Wings of Love *by Stephen Pearson. Throughout the following, Angela monitors Laurence's pulse.*] Get me something for his head. And get his feet up higher. No, that's too big.

BEVERLY: What's going on? What's the matter with him? Mind, Sue. Laurence! What's happened, Ang, has he passed out? Laurence!

SUSAN: Tony, can you lift his feet?

BEVERLY: Tony!

[*Tony and Susan see to Laurence's feet.*]

Sue, go and get him a glass of water, quickly, please. Now, Laurence, come on, you're all right, come on, Laurence, Laurence!

ANGELA: No, leave him.

TONY: Leave him.

BEVERLY: Actually, Angela, he happens to be my husband, all right?

ANGELA: Yeah, but we've got to let him breathe.

BEVERLY: Yeah, well, he is breathing, for Christ's sake.

BEVERLY ⎫ [*shaking him*]: Laurence, come on, come on!!
ANGELA ⎭ : Can you get an ambulance, instead of sitting there?

TONY: Ambulance?

ANGELA: Yes!

SUSAN: Beverly, leave him alone!

BEVERLY: All right, then, Angela, what is the matter with him?

ANGELA: I think he's had a heart attack.

TONY: Where's your phone?

BEVERLY: A heart attack, Ang?

TONY: Where's your phone?

BEVERLY: Under the bar. Ang, are you sure?

ANGELA: He hasn't got false teeth, has he?

BEVERLY: No, of course he hasn't got false teeth! Ang, look his lips are going all blue, look.

ANGELA: Don't worry.

BEVERLY: Ang, his hands are going freezing.

ANGELA [to Susan]: Can you get him a blanket or something to keep him warm?

  [Exit Susan.]

BEVERLY: Laurence ... Now, Laurence. Can he hear me, d'you think, Ang?

ANGELA: Yes.

BEVERLY: Yeah. Laurence, Laurence.

ANGELA: No, leave him, he's got to lie still!

BEVERLY: Oh, Christ, Ang!

  [Beverly gets up, goes to the bar, and pours herself a brandy.]

ANGELA: Have you got through yet?

TONY: I'm trying to get a bloody line.

  [Susan has come back, with a duvet. She covers Laurence with it.]

BEVERLY: Ang, his face is going all blue, look!

TONY: Ambulance.

ANGELA: Tell them it's urgent.

TONY: What? Someone turn that fucking record off! Er – 503-9041.

  [Susan turns off the record.]

BEVERLY: Ang, Ang. Listen to that noise he's making.

TONY: Hullo, er, could we have an ambulance, please? [Pause.] What's the number of your house? What's the number of your HOUSE?!

SUSAN: Er – thirteen!

BEVERLY: Thirteen, thirteen.

TONY: 13, Richmond Road.

  [For the rest of the telephone conversation that follows, Tony and Beverly can overlap slightly.]

BEVERLY: Angela, I told him this would happen.

TONY: Er, he's had a heart attack.

BEVERLY: I said to him, Laurence, you're going to have a heart attack.

TONY: 503-9041.

BEVERLY: But he wouldn't listen to me, Ang.

TONY: That's right, yeah.

BEVERLY: But I never thought it would happen at this age; I thought it'll be more when he was fifty or sixty.

TONY: Thank you.

[*Tony hangs up.*]

BEVERLY: Oh, Christ, Christ, Sue, listen to that noise he's making, Sue!!

SUSAN: Angela, is there anything we can do?

ANGELA: No, we must just wait for the ambulance.

[*Beverly lights a cigarette.*]

BEVERLY: Ang, what happens when they get him to the hospital? Will they give him oxygen to revive him?

ANGELA: They've got everything he needs in the ambulance.

BEVERLY: Yeah?

[*Susan is putting away the Beethoven.*]

Oh, Christ! [*She goes back to the bar for more brandy.*] Sue, d'you want a little drop of brandy?

SUSAN: No, thank you.

BEVERLY: Tone?

TONY: No, thank you!

BEVERLY ⎫
              ⎬ : Ang, d'you want a little drop of brandy?
ANGELA ⎭   No, no.

BEVERLY: Now, Ang, listen to me ... d'you think it would be a good idea if I put a little dab of brandy on his lips?

ANGELA: No!

BEVERLY: Now I don't mean for him to drink it – no? Well, how about a little dab of water, then, eh?

ANGELA: No, he must just lie still.

BEVERLY: Well, shall I get a cold flannel and lay it across his forehead?

ANGELA: He'll be all right if he lies still.

BEVERLY [*kneeling*]: 'Cos I am very fond of him, you know, Ang.

TONY: Keep that cigarette out of his face!

BEVERLY: All right, Tony, lay off me if you don't mind, please!

SUSAN: Beverly, you're flicking ash all over him!

BEVERLY: All right, Sue, that'll do from you as well!

SUSAN: Calm down!

BEVERLY: Look, Sue: it's all right for you, your husband isn't lying here with a heart attack, is he?

SUSAN: Angela, is there nothing we can do?

ANGELA: No! Just sit down.

[*Susan sits.*]

BEVERLY: It's my fault, isn't it? I know it is, Ang. But, I didn't mean to upset him tonight, I didn't, Sue, I wouldn't do that. But, Sue, he is argumentative with me. And when he shouts, I can't help but shout back; but I didn't mean to upset him tonight. You see, and when he started talking about his pictures, I should have kept quiet, but I couldn't. And I shouldn't have brought that picture down, Sue, 'cos he hates that picture. [*Pause.*] Oh, Christ, this is ridiculous! Tony, where's that ambulance? Ang, shall we give them a ring again?

SUSAN: Beverly, we've only just phoned them!

BEVERLY: I know we've only just phoned them, Sue, but you don't know what's going on at these places, they could have taken the address down wrong, or anything – they might go to the wrong road for all we know! Tony, do me a favour, get on the phone, and just check what's going on, please!

TONY: Shall I ring them again, Ang?

BEVERLY: Look, never mind her, I know she's a nurse, but I happen to be his bloody wife!

TONY: All right!

BEVERLY: Now get on the phone!

[*Tony dials 999. Beverly sits.*]

SUSAN: How is he?

ANGELA: He's all right.

BEVERLY: Mind you, Sue: he's brought this on himself. I'm sorry, but he has. If you knew, Sue, the number of times I have pleaded with him to take a day off and relax, and he wouldn't – he wouldn't listen to me, Sue. He wouldn't take any notice of me, Sue! And d'you know why? Because basically he's stubborn, and he's pig-headed!!!

TONY: Ambulance. 503–9041. Yes.

BEVERLY: 13 Richmond Road, tell 'em, Tony, and it's off Ravensway. Make sure they've got it right.

TONY: Hallo – er, we phoned for an ambulance earlier, and it doesn't seem to have arrived.

BEVERLY: Listen, Tony, tell them we've been waiting for ten minutes actually and there's a man lying here with a heart attack.

TONY: Shut up!!!

SUSAN: Beverly. BE QUIET!!!

BEVERLY: I beg your pardon, Sue?

SUSAN: Will you just shut up for a minute?

BEVERLY: Look, Sue, I'm telling you now: this is my house, and if you don't like it, piss off!

ANGELA: Oh, shut up, please.

TONY: 13 Richmond Road. 503–9041. Ta. Thank you.

[*Tony hangs up.*]

BEVERLY: What did they say, Tone?

TONY: It's on its way.

BEVERLY: Great.

[*Pause. The shrieking voices of a few teenage girls are heard in the street. Then the Rock music from the party starts again.*]

Oh, for God's sake, Sue; would you go down and tell Abigail?

SUSAN: It's not my fault they're making such a row.

BEVERLY: I know, Sue, but she's your daughter, isn't she?

SUSAN: Well, I can't help that! Can I use the phone?

BEVERLY: Yeah, go on.

ANGELA: Now it's all right – just lie still.

[*Laurence has started to come round.*]

BEVERLY: What is it, Ang? Is he coming round a little bit, is he?

ANGELA: Yeah. You're gonna be fine – keep still.

BEVERLY: Now, Laurence. Laurence, it's Beverly speaking! Now, listen to me, Laurence. I'm just putting me cigarette down, 'cos we don't want to blow smoke in your face, do we? Now, listen to me, Laurence. Now, Laurence, you're not well. You're gonna be all right, we're gonna take you to the hospital – now listen to me ... I'm gonna stay with you all the time, Laurence, and I'm not gonna leave you, all right? Now Ang is looking after you, see?

[*Angela is now pounding Laurence's chest, Laurence having died at about the point where Beverly was saying, 'I'm just putting me cigarette down'.*]

Ang! Ang, what're you doing?

SUSAN: Could I speak to Abigail, please?

Abigail!

Abigail Lawson!

[*Angela listens to Laurence's chest. Then she starts to administer the kiss-of-life. Then she stops.*]

ANGELA: Tony, can you hold my hair out of my face?

TONY: Eh?

ANGELA: Tony!

[*Tony crosses, and holds Angela's hair out of the way, while she does the*

kiss-of-life. This goes on for some time. Eventually, she gives up. Tony lets
go of her hair. She sinks back against an armchair.
Pause.
Beverly throws her arms round Tony with a gasp, holding the embrace.
Pause.
Angela leaps up suddenly, grasping one leg.]
  Ur, shit! Ur, Tony, Tony. Tony!
    [*Angela flies across the room. Tony disengages himself from Beverly.*]
TONY: What's the matter? You haven't got cramp again, have you?
  Come here – give us your leg! Stretch it. Stretch it!
    [*Angela is relieved, and lies still on the floor. Tony kneels in exhaustion.*
    Beverly sobs.]
SUSAN: Abigail, it's Mummy here.
  Abigail?
  ABIGAIL!!
    [*Blackout.*
    The Rock music surges.]

CURTAIN

GOOSE-PIMPLES

First performed at the Hampstead Theatre, London, on 3 March 1981, when the cast was as follows:

VERNON	*Jim Broadbent*
JACKIE	*Marion Bailey*
IRVING	*Paul Jesson*
FRANKIE	*Jill Baker*
MUHAMMAD	*Antony Sher*

By Mike Leigh
Designed by Caroline Beaver
Lighting by Alan O'Toole

The same production opened at the Garrick Theatre, London, on 29 April 1981.

Goose-Pimples was evolved from scratch entirely by rehearsal through improvisation.

The action takes place in Vernon's flat.

ACT I
Scene 1   Late spring. Early morning
Scene 2   Two days later. Early evening
Scene 3   Later the same evening

ACT II
A few minutes later

Time – the present

NOTE

The Arabic in this text has not been expressed phonetically. We have kept to the standard spelling, as used by the Linguaphone Institute.

It is therefore essential for actors playing Muhammad to consult Arabic speakers for the Arabic pronunciation itself, and, if possible, Saudi Nationals for the pronunciation of the English.

The following are the names of towns and villages in Saudi Arabia referred to by Muhammad: Abha, Arafat, Dhahran, Jiddha (Jeddah), Mecca, Mina, Muzdalifah, Taif.

ACT I

SCENE 1

Vernon's flat. An early morning in late spring.

The flat is on the second floor of a block of flats purpose-built around 1935. The lounge and dining areas are in a double room, which was designed originally as two rooms with folding doors between them, but the doors have been removed. In the lounge area are a black leather sofa and swivel armchair, a side table, a bar with bar-stools, a music centre with cassettes and records underneath, a television and an imitation leopard-skin rug. In the dining area, there are four chrome dining chairs, a table and a wall-unit, on the shelves of which are a few paperbacks, two or three small school sports trophies and a telephone. The walls are papered with tiger-skin wallpaper (or something similar). There are no pictures, but several mirrors and veteran car motifs. The doors to the two areas are close to each other, and have frosted-glass panes. On the door in the dining area, one of the panes has been replaced at some time by a clear pane. Across the hall is the kitchenette, a small part of which is visible. The front door and the other rooms cannot be seen.

When the CURTAIN rises, the room is empty.

Vernon enters, wearing a track suit. He is out of breath, and is sweating a little. He picks up an executive case from a bar-stool. He puts it on the dining-table, and opens it. He takes out a diary. He takes the telephone from the wall-unit, and puts it on the table. He flicks through the diary.

Jackie enters.

JACKIE: Hi.

VERNON: Good morning, Jackie. How are you?

JACKIE: All right. Been jogging?

VERNON: Indeed I have. Still up? [*He dials.*]

JACKIE: Yeh. I don't really feel tired this morning. We had a really busy night, you know – you don't want to go to bed when you get back.

VERNON: No?

JACKIE: Had your shower yet?

VERNON: No – just making a quick phone call.

JACKIE: Oh. I might have a bath. Is that a business call?

VERNON: Yeh.

JACKIE: Oh, really? 'S a bit early.

VERNON: It's the only time I can get hold of this geezer.

JACKIE: I know, it's the best time to get 'em, you know – when they're not expecting it.

VERNON: It was his idea I should call at this ungodly hour.

JACKIE: Oh, really?

VERNON: I've got a feeling he wants to cancel his order – got fed up with waiting.

JACKIE: What was it, another Metro?

VERNON: Yes. Started talking about getting a Datsun now, hasn't he.

JACKIE: 'Ow long's 'e been waiting, then?

VERNON: Nine weeks now.

JACKIE: 'T's bad, init? Makes you look stupid, you know.

VERNON: Not bloody kidding it makes me look stupid – always ends up on our bloody doorstep, I tell you.

JACKIE: That's right. It's a nice little car, though, a Metro. 'T's perky, you know?

VERNON: Try again. [*He dials again.*]

JACKIE: It's not really a status car, though, is it?

VERNON: So you're working Saturday night, are you?

JACKIE: That's right – well I'm on early shift, you know?
       [*Pause.*]
    Is your girlfriend coming over, as well?

VERNON: No – just a threesome.

JACKIE: Oh, really?

VERNON: She's going down to Swindon for the weekend.

JACKIE: What's she going down there for?

VERNON: She's taking her kiddy down to see his dad.

JACKIE: Oh, really? That's a bit of a drag for her, init?

VERNON: Suppose so. It's not my problem.

JACKIE: No, that's right. It don't pay to get too involved, you know.

VERNON: [*into the receiver*]: Come on!

JACKIE: Who's doing the cooking, then?

VERNON: Yours truly.

JACKIE: Oh, really?

VERNON: I'm quite a good chef, Jackie.

JACKIE: Oh. What you 'avin?

VERNON: Steak.

JACKIE: Oh, yeh ... well, you can't go wrong with steak, y'know?

VERNON: What time d'you finish Saturday night?

JACKIE: Ten.

VERNON: You're very welcome to join us for a drink if you get back in time.

JACKIE: Oh, thanks, yeh – well, I don't really know yet, you know, I
   might be going on somewhere with some friends after work, probably
   go to a club or something, go out for a meal.
VERNON: Feel free.
JACKIE: Mm. Your friends goin'a be stayin' late?
VERNON: I should imagine so, knowing these two.
JACKIE: Oh, really?
VERNON: More than likely outstay their welcome.
JACKIE: Oh, well, you just got to tell people.
   [*Vernon slams down the receiver and paces round the room, thrusting at the air
   with a squash-racket he has picked up.*]
VERNON: Oh, for Christ's sake, what's the bloody point! Tells me to
   phone, then he's not sodding there!
JACKIE: It's bad business. I mean you're doin' 'im a favour.
VERNON: I don't exactly enjoy starting work an hour and a half early,
   I can tell you.
JACKIE: No, 't's right.
   [*Vernon puts the telephone away, puts the diary back in the case, and puts
   the case on the floor in the corner.*]
   D'you play squash last night?
VERNON: Yes.
JACKIE: D'you lose again?
VERNON: No, I won, as it happens.
JACKIE: Oh, did you? What did your friend say?
VERNON: He paid up, didn't he?
JACKIE: 'T's right. 'E's got to, 'asn't 'e? If that's the agreement. You
   know, it's like business.
VERNON: You're right, Jackie. You don't know how right you are.
   [*Vernon exits to his room, taking his squash-racket with him.*]
JACKIE: These blokes, they say they're goin' to do something, and when
   it comes to the crunch, they back out. Thing is, Vern, if you think
   someone's going to pull a stroke like that, you've got to tell 'em where
   you stand, straight off. They may not like it, but the end justifies the
   means.
VERNON [*off*]: That's right.
JACKIE: Yeh, you've just got to be straight with people. Especially if
   there's a lot of big money changing hands. It's only good sense in the
   long run. You get these cowboys, but let's face it, anyone with a bit
   of savvy's not going to get stung twice, are they?
VERNON [*off*]: No.
JACKIE: I mean, once you've 'ad a bit of experience in selling, you can

recognize a duff customer; you've just got to be straight with 'em, you know, say, 'Look, don't waste my time, and I won't waste yours, right?' Yeh, you've really got to believe in your product, you know, when you're selling, got to be a bit pushy, yeh? I don't mean pressurize people, but you've got to be positive. It's no use askin' if they want to buy, you've got to tell 'em they do want to buy, I mean, you're doin' them a favour, really. Yeh, it's all about S A T O C, you know.

VERNON [off]: You what?

JACKIE: SATOC, yeh? You gotta Show the Advantage of your product, Turn the customer's Objections, and Close the sale. SATOC, yeh? S–A–T–O–C.

VERNON [off]: Oh, by the way, Jackie – when can you let me have the rent?

JACKIE: When d'you wannit?

VERNON [off]: It was due last Sunday.

JACKIE: Yes, well, I haven't really seen you, you know?

VERNON [off]: Write us out a cheque, leave it on the table.

JACKIE: Yeh, all right!

> [*Jackie goes into the hall quickly. She exits into her own room, and slams the door.*
> *The lights quickly fade to a Blackout.*]

SCENE 2

The same. Two days later. Early evening.

> *Vernon enters, dressed informally, with a tray of nuts. He makes several trips to the kitchen for the rest of the food.*
>
> *He puts on a Rod Stewart record, then goes to the wall-unit and takes out cutlery, glasses, etc. He sets the table for three, quickly and efficiently, putting a plate of melon and a dinner roll at each place. Then he pours himself a whisky and settles down with it at the bar. The doorbell rings immediately. Vernon lowers the volume of the music, and then goes into the hall.*
>
> *He exits to answer the front door.*

VERNON [off]: Hello!

IRVING [off]: Hello, Vernon.

> [*Irving enters with a bottle of red wine (wrapped).*]

VERNON [off]: Hello, Frankie – very glad you could make it.

FRANKIE [off]: Are you?

> [*The front door closes.*]

IRVING: Got a bottle of wine for you, Vernon – here you are.

[*Frankie and Vernon enter.*]

FRANKIE: Oh, what a super flat!

VERNON [*unwrapping the bottle*]: Oh, you shouldn't have bothered!

IRVING: Oh, I see, you've got a choice of doors, then, have you, eh?

VERNON: Yes, this room has a divide facility, an option I chose not to take up.

IRVING: Oh, really?

VERNON: I just whipped the dividing doors out.

FRANKIE: Well, it gives the illusion of it being bigger than it is, doesn't it, Ver?

VERNON: Frankie – let me take your coat.

FRANKIE: Thank you.

IRVING: [*looking at the walls*]: I've never seen anything like this before, Vernon.

VERNON: The wallpaper? Yes, I'm quite pleased with it.

IRVING: Did you shoot it yourself, eh?

[*Vernon and Irving laugh uproariously.*
Vernon exits with Frankie's coat.]

FRANKIE [*inspecting the table*]: Oh, this looks nice, doesn't it?

IRVING: So this is the famous bar, then, is it, eh?

[*Vernon enters.*]

VERNON: Yes – it's a little bit special, isn't it?

IRVING: It certainly is.

VERNON: And you've got to admit it's me.

IRVING: All you need now is the barmaid to go with it, eh?

VERNON: No shortage of barmaids here, Irving, I can assure you of that!

IRVING: I'm sure there's not, no!

[*Vernon and Irving laugh uproariously.*]

FRANKIE: Of course, we wouldn't be happy with a small flat, would we, darling?

VERNON: As a matter of fact, Frankie, it's a very spacious flat, and I personally don't feel cramped in any way.

FRANKIE: No.

VERNON: And it certainly fulfils my every requirement to the letter.

IRVING: And we all know about your requirements, don't we, eh?

[*Vernon and Irving laugh uproariously.*]

VERNON: Frankie – would you like to sit down, make yourself comfortable?

FRANKIE: Thank you. [*She sits down on the sofa.*]

IRVING: I hope the wine fits in with the menu, Vernon.

VERNON: Oh, I'm sure it will, Irving.

IRVING: Should be warm enough – I was holding it between my thighs in the car. [*He laughs uproariously.*]

    [*Frankie takes out a cigarette.*]

VERNON: Frankie – let me give you a light. There you are. [*He lights her cigarette.*]

FRANKIE: Thank you.

VERNON: Get you an ashtray. [*He places one next to her.*]

FRANKIE: Thank you.

VERNON: Frankie: what can I get you to drink?

FRANKIE: Bacardi-and-Coke, please, Ver.

VERNON: Bacardi I do not have.

IRVING: Oh, caught him out, have you?

FRANKIE: Oh, it doesn't matter – I'll have a gin-and-tonic.

VERNON: Gin-and-tonic. Same for you, Irving, if I'm not very much mistaken?

IRVING: As per usual – you know my tastes, eh?

VERNON: Indeed I do.

    [*Vernon and Irving laugh uproariously. Pause. Frankie utters a subconscious, but quite loud, monosyllabic 'Oh!'; this means, vaguely, a combination of 'Well, here we all are!' and 'Oh, dear, isn't life painful?' Hereafter, 'Frankie utters' refers to this ejaculation.*]

IRVING: Well, this is cosy.

VERNON [*pouring the drinks*]: So, you managed to find the old place all right, then?

FRANKIE: No problem at all, Ver.

IRVING: I thought it was wise to give the North Circular a miss.

FRANKIE: I was driving.

VERNON: Were you, Frankie?

FRANKIE: I was.

IRVING: Yes, we had to come in Frankie's car.

VERNON: Oh, what's wrong with the Metro this time?

IRVING: Couldn't get it started.

VERNON: Done it again, have you, Irving?

IRVING: No, carburettor's on the blink – I shall have to swap it next week.

VERNON: What are you going to swap it for?

IRVING: Dunno ... That Applejack HLE.

FRANKIE: Oh, no – not Applejack!

IRVING: What?

VERNON: Too late – I've sold it.

IRVING: When?

VERNON: First thing this morning.

IRVING: You move fast – who to?

VERNON: Our friend Mr Tench.

IRVING: I thought he'd decided he was getting a Datsun.

VERNON: So did he till I changed his mind for him. Ice, Frankie?

FRANKIE: Please.

IRVING: Well, you've got him off your back at last, anyway.

VERNON: You're not bloody kidding, Irving. [*He hands out the drinks.*]

IRVING: You've certainly got yourself well set up here, Vernon.

FRANKIE: There's a nasty smell on your stairs, Ver.

VERNON: No, no, Frankie, that's just the fluid the cleaners use.

FRANKIE: Oh. Smells a bit like a public lavatory to me.

VERNON: Is that a fact, Frankie? I don't frequent public lavatories [*Offering a tray of nuts*] Can I tempt you?

IRVING: You don't want to pick anything up, do you?
     [*Vernon and Irving laugh uproariously.*]

VERNON [*sitting down*]: No, as a matter of fact, under the terms of the lease, the management are required to keep the common parts of these flats – the stairwells, the halls and forecourts, and the parking area – in an orderly and hygienic condition, and I must say, to their eternal credit, this is adhered to, which I think you'll agree is a blessing in these days of shoddy workmanship and poor service.

FRANKIE: There's not much parking space, though, is there?

VERNON: You park at the front, did you?

FRANKIE: Mm.

VERNON: Yes, it's sometimes a bit tricky at the front, but there's ample facility at the rear.

IRVING: Bit like Raquel Welch, eh?

FRANKIE: Why don't you come and sit down, darling?

IRVING: Ample facility at the rear, eh?
     [*Vernon and Irving laugh uproariously.*]

VERNON: Well, I must say, it's nice to see you again, Frankie.

FRANKIE: It's nice to see you, too, Ver.

VERNON: And how've you been?

FRANKIE: Absolutely fine, thank you.

VERNON: Oh, what've you been up to?

FRANKIE: Well, we've been terribly busy, haven't we, darling?

IRVING: Oh, yes – very active, eh? [*He laughs uproariously.*]

FRANKIE: We've been eating out a tremendous amount.

IRVING: That's right.

FRANKIE: Socializing – you know?

VERNON: Oh, yes?

FRANKIE: Seeing a lot of our friends.

VERNON: Oh, jolly good.

IRVING: Who?

FRANKIE: Sit down, sweetheart. And how have you been, Ver?

VERNON: Oh, very well indeed, Frankie. These last few weeks I've been rushed off my feet, I can't tell you.

FRANKIE: I'm sure you have.

IRVING: Who've we been seeing, then?

FRANKIE: Eh?

IRVING: Who've we been seeing?

FRANKIE: Then of course we're going on our holidays soon, aren't we?

IRVING [*sitting next to Frankie on the sofa*]: We haven't been seeing anybody.

FRANKIE: Aren't we?

IRVING: What?

FRANKIE: Going on our holiday in five weeks?

IRVING: Oh, yeh, Corfu.

FRANKIE: That's right.

IRVING: Five weeks today, and we'll be there.

VERNON: Yes, yes; that sounds very exciting.

FRANKIE: We're looking forward to it, aren't we?

IRVING: We certainly are – all those beach balls bouncing around, eh? [*He laughs uproariously.*]

VERNON: Cheers!

IRVING ⎫
FRANKIE ⎭ [*together*]: Cheers!

VERNON: And welcome to my humble abode, such as it is. It's very nice to have you both here at long last.

IRVING: It's very nice to be here, at long last.

FRANKIE: Darling – your hair's sticking up again.

IRVING: That's not all that's sticking up, eh? [*He laughs uproariously.*]

VERNON: No, I must say I envy you your holiday plans, but I never go away in the summer. I take a few days off during Wimbledon fortnight, which is something I enjoy, but, unlike Irving here, I can't justify turning my back on the busiest period of the year, profit-wise.

IRVING: Oh, no: August is when it really picks up – we'll be back long before then.

VERNON: No, no, Irving; the time to sell a motor car is from May to

September – that's when people want to buy. It's a well-known fact, Frankie.

IRVING: Don't listen to him – he doesn't know what he's talking about.

FRANKIE: We can afford our holiday, Ver.

VERNON: I'm sure you can, Frankie, and your financial affairs are none of my business. Would you like a nibble? [*He offers the nuts.*]

IRVING: Oh. I'll have a nibble. Eh? [*He laughs uproariously.*]

    [*Frankie eats some nuts.*]

VERNON: Why don't you just hang on to those, Frankie? No, I take my major break in the winter, which, I think you'll agree, is the time to get away from this God-forsaken climate.

IRVING: Well, this is it.

FRANKIE: We had a winter holiday once, didn't we, sweetheart?

VERNON: Oh, yes – you went ski-ing.

FRANKIE: That's right.

VERNON: Yes. Irving's told me about that.

FRANKIE: Oh, has he? What did you tell him?

IRVING: Well . . . we had a good time. Didn't we?

FRANKIE: Oh yes, it was absolutely super. I love ski-ing.

    [*Vernon and Irving laugh uproariously.*]

VERNON: Yes, but it's not the same as getting away to the sun, though, is it?

FRANKIE: Well, you'd be surprised, Ver; you can get a super sun-tan on top of the Alps, you know.

IRVING: Oh, yes: the sun reflects off the snow every bit as much as it does off the sand.

FRANKIE: That's right.

VERNON: Ah, yes; but it doesn't compare with lying back on the beach, soaking up the sun, with that wonderful aroma of Ambre Solaire hanging on the breeze.

FRANKIE: No, and that's exactly why we don't go away in the winter any more. We've been going to Ibiza for a few years, haven't we, sweetheart?

IRVING: Mm.

FRANKIE: But, to be absolutely honest with you, Ver, it has got a bit crowded recently.

IRVING: Yes, we've given up Ibiza as a bad job, you know.

FRANKIE: That's right.

IRVING: It's become overrun with Germans.

VERNON: Oh, no, no, no. I can't be doing with the Germans. The only kind of German I like is blonde, nubile, preferably on its back, and of the female variety.

[*Vernon and Irving laugh uproariously.*]

IRVING: And how is Astrid, by the way?

VERNON: Very well indeed, thank you, Irving.

IRVING: Good.

FRANKIE: Who's that, then, Ver?

VERNON: A young friend of mine.

FRANKIE: Oh, yes?

IRVING: What's she up to tonight, then, eh?

VERNON: Looking after the kiddies, I expect.

FRANKIE: Oh, she's got kids, has she?

IRVING: No – she's an au pair Vernon picked up.

VERNON: She's a young German girl, she's working over here, she hasn't got many friends, so I took it upon myself to – shall we say? – entertain her.

IRVING: Show her the sights, eh?

[*Vernon and Irving laugh uproariously.*]

FRANKIE: How old is she, Ver?

VERNON: Why do you ask, Frankie?

FRANKIE: I was just wondering.

VERNON: She's eighteen.

FRANKIE: Bit young for you, isn't it?

VERNON: It's legal, Frankie. And let's face it, these young girls can teach us older men a thing or two.

IRVING: The younger ones refresh the parts the older ones cannot reach, eh?

[*Vernon and Irving laugh uproariously.*]

VERNON: Like it! Like it!

IRVING: And, talking of which, how's the lodger, by the way?

VERNON: She's fine, thank you, Irving.

IRVING: Fitting in well, is she?

VERNON: No problems at all.

IRVING: And how are you fitting in with her, then, eh?

VERNON: I don't see what you're driving at, Irving.

IRVING: Oh, come on, Vernon!

VERNON: No, no, no, you've lost me completely. The arrangement I have with my lodger is strictly business.

FRANKIE: Oh, really?

VERNON: I don't mix business with pleasure, Frankie.

FRANKIE: No.

VERNON: It's not advisable, no matter how attractive the prospect may seem.

[*Irving picks up the nude statuette.*]

IRVING: Is this your mascot, then, Vernon, eh?

VERNON: Careful, Irving – that's an *objet d'art*, for Christ's sake!

FRANKIE: Put it down, darling, please.

IRVING: Very nice, isn't it? Eh? I shall have to get one of these – in the flesh. [*He puts the statuette back.*]

VERNON: I thought you had one.

IRVING: Yeh. Well . . . not quite this shape, eh? [*He laughs uproariously.*]

FRANKIE: There's no need to be rude, Irving.

[*Pause.*]

She's a croupier, isn't she, your lodger?

IRVING ⎫[*together*]: Yes, she is.
VERNON ⎭   That's right.

FRANKIE: Now, that wouldn't suit me.

VERNON: No?

FRANKIE: No. Because, quite frankly, Ver, I don't altogether approve of gambling.

VERNON: Don't you, Frankie?

FRANKIE: No. So I wouldn't want to put myself in a position whereby I was encouraging it in any way.

IRVING: Oh, yeh? And what sort of position is that, then, eh? [*He laughs uproariously.*]

FRANKIE: No, and I have to say, Ver, I think it's immoral.

VERNON: It's a free country, Frankie, and I think we ought to leave it up to the individual to make up his or her own mind with regard to this one.

FRANKIE: Oh, of course – each to his own.

IRVING: Yeh, but only as a last resort, eh? [*He laughs uproariously.*]

FRANKIE: No, the fact is, though, Ver, I couldn't actually stand all those men oggling at me all the time, either.

IRVING: Well, they wouldn't be looking at you, anyway. [*Getting up*] Come on, Vernon, let's have a look around the flat, see what you've made of the place.

[*Irving goes into the hall and exits towards Vernon's bedroom.*]

VERNON [*getting up*]: Yes, of course, Irving. Frankie, would you like to have a look around?

FRANKIE: I wouldn't mind.

[*Vernon leans over Frankie from behind, and puts his hand on her breast.*]

[*Getting up*] I don't know how you can do that, Ver.

[*Frankie goes into the hall, followed by Vernon.*

Frankie exits to the kitchen.
 Vernon exits to his bedroom.]

IRVING [*off*]: Good suspension on the bed, Vernon.

VERNON [*off*]: Oh, you've found my bedroom, have you, Irving?

IRVING [*off*]: Yes!

VERNON [*off*]: Yes, it's a good bed!

IRVING [*off*]: Nice big one, eh?

VERNON [*off*]: Well – the bigger the better!

IRVING [*off*]: Yes, that's what I always say!

 [*Vernon and Irving laugh uproariously, off.*]

FRANKIE [*off*]: Your kitchen's a bit cramped, Vernon.

 [*Irving crosses the hall and goes towards Jackie's room.*]

IRVING [*off*]: Is this the lodger's room, then, Vernon?

 [*Vernon appears in the hall.*]

VERNON: I don't think you need to go in there, Irving.

 [*Frankie comes out of the kitchen and starts to follow Irving.*]

FRANKIE: Oh, I'm sure she wouldn't mind, being as you've got such a good business relationship.

VERNON: No, the point is, Frankie, the agreement I have with my lodger is that we respect each other's privacy – it's as simple as that.

FRANKIE: Well, I only want a little peep.

 [*Frankie exits towards Jackie's room.*]

VERNON: Frankie, please!

FRANKIE [*off*]: Oh, Christ! She isn't very tidy, is she?

VERNON [*moving into the lounge*]: Whether she's tidy or not is of no concern to me. What Jackie does in her own room is her business. As long as she's tidy around the rest of the flat, that's all I ask.

 [*Frankie enters.*]

FRANKIE [*as she enters*]: Now, don't get me wrong, Ver – I didn't mean to intrude.

VERNON: I'm sorry, Frankie. And I certainly didn't mean to infer that you were a snoop.

FRANKIE: So, what have you been up to, eh?

VERNON: Oh, you know. This and that.

FRANKIE: No, I don't know. That's why I'm asking.

VERNON: I don't know what you're talking about.

FRANKIE: Been having a good social life, have you?

VERNON: Oh, I can't complain. Shall we eat? Would you like to sit here, Frankie?

FRANKIE: Thank you. [*She sits at the table.*] I must say I am feeling rather hungry.

VERNON: You're looking rather tasty.

> [*Vernon exits to the kitchen.*
> *Frankie butters her roll busily and proceeds to eat it avidly.*
> *Vernon enters with an opened bottle of white wine.*]

Oh, yes. I see what you mean. You are a hungry girl.

FRANKIE: Why didn't you phone me?

VERNON: I'm sorry, Frankie?

FRANKIE: You never phoned me up.

VERNON: Oh, that! Oh, you want to talk about it now, do you? This is an ideal moment, isn't it? Why don't we just wait for Irving? Where is Irving, by the way? Is he going to join us later? Is that the plan?

> [*Frankie gets up and goes to the door.*]

FRANKIE: Irving!

IRVING [*off*]: What? Oh, yes – just coming!

FRANKIE: What are you up to?

> [*Irving enters.*]

IRVING: Nothing. What's the matter?

FRANKIE [*caressing his hair*]: Nothing, darling. Sit down.

IRVING: Don't do that!

VERNON: Irving, would you like to sit here?

IRVING: Oh, right, thank you. [*He sits down.*]

FRANKIE [*sitting*]: D'you mind if I start, Ver?

VERNON [*sitting*]: No, by all means, Frankie, tuck in! [*He pours the wine.*]

IRVING: This looks nice.

FRANKIE: Got any ginger, Ver?

VERNON: Ginger? No.

IRVING: Oh, you have to have ginger on melon, you know.

FRANKIE: Oh, yes: it complements the flavour.

VERNON: Is that a fact? Well, that's very interesting. I didn't know that.

FRANKIE: Well, you'll remember next time.

VERNON: Yes. Ginger and melon. Well, I've learned something new this evening, haven't I? That's an added bonus, isn't it?

IRVING: Is she a tall girl, Vernon?

VERNON: Is who a tall girl, Irving?

IRVING: Jackie.

VERNON: No, she's not, as it happens.

IRVING: She's as tall as you, though, isn't she?

VERNON: Irving, I'm six-foot-two. If Jackie was six-foot-two, I would say, without any doubt, she was a tall girl.

IRVING: Yeh, well, I've seen some tall girls in my time, eh? [*He laughs uproariously.*]

VERNON: I'm sure you have. As a matter of fact, Jackie's quite petite.

IRVING: Oh. I could have sworn she'd be tall.

VERNON: You like tall girls, do you, Irving?

FRANKIE: I'm five-foot-seven, Ver.

VERNON: Yes, of course, you're a tall girl, aren't you, Frankie?

FRANKIE: I'm five-foot-seven, Ir, but I'm not six-foot-two, and if I was six-foot-two, I wouldn't just be tall, I'd be huge. Stupid bugger.

VERNON: Mind you, you are quite a big girl, aren't you, Frankie?

FRANKIE: And what exactly do you mean by that, Vernon?

VERNON: Would you like some sugar on your melon?

FRANKIE: No, thank you. We have it quite a lot, don't we, darling?

IRVING: Yeh, we do, don't we, eh!

[*Vernon and Irving laugh uproariously.*]

FRANKIE: Melon!

IRVING: Yeh – I know!

FRANKIE: I like to ring the changes.

VERNON: I imagine you have ginger on it, though, don't you?

IRVING: Yeh, we do – sprinkled all over it! [*He laughs uproariously.*]

FRANKIE: It's a nice ripe one, this, isn't it?

IRVING: Yeh. Here, Vernon: do you know how to buy a melon in the greengrocer's? You have to give it a squeeze to see if it's ripe; you push the end in with your finger, and if it gives just a little bit, you know it's ready!

[*Vernon and Irving laugh uproariously.*]

FRANKIE: Oh, please! [*She finishes her melon.*]

[*Pause. Frankie utters her noise, q.v.*]

VERNON: My word, that slipped down very easily, didn't it, Frankie?

IRVING: Not half as it slips up! [*He laughs uproariously.*]

FRANKIE: Have you got any more, Ver?

VERNON: Yes, of course, Frankie – I'm sorry, I should've remembered: the ever-open door! Irving, would you like some more?

IRVING: Oh, yes, please – thank you.

[*Vernon takes their plates and exits to the kitchen.*]

FRANKIE: Can I give you a hand?

[*Frankie exits to the kitchen.*
Inaudibly off: 'Why didn't you phone me?'
Vernon enters, with more melon, followed by Frankie.]

I asked you a question.

VERNON: I'm sorry, Frankie, what question was that? I was miles away – I must have been thinking about something else. Here you are, Irving.

IRVING: Oh, thank you.

VERNON: Frankie just asked me a question.

IRVING: Oh?

VERNON: Come on, Frankie, sit down. You've got a lot to get through. More wine, Irving?

IRVING: Yes, please.

VERNON [*pouring the wine*]: It's not a bad wine, is it?

IRVING: No.

VERNON: As a light, fruity wine, I find it most acceptable. It's certainly one of my standbys.

FRANKIE: It's a bit dry.

VERNON: It is a little dry, yes, but I like a dry wine. Perhaps that's just one of the hazards of having a sophisticated palate. Who knows?

IRVING: She is a redhead, though, isn't she?

VERNON: Is who a redhead, Irving?

IRVING: Jackie.

VERNON: No, Jackie is not a redhead, and she's not six-foot-two. She's a petite brunette. Compris? Now, if you'll excuse me, I'll go and get on with the main course.

　　[*Vernon exits to the kitchen.*]

FRANKIE: What's the matter with you?

IRVING: Eh?

FRANKIE: Oh, for Christ's sake. [*She crosses to her bag and takes out a cigarette.*]

IRVING: Having an inter-course cigarette, then, are you, eh? [*He laughs uproariously.*]

FRANKIE: Yes, that's right, Irving.

　　[*Irving continues to snigger. Pause. Frankie inspects the room.*]
　　It's all a bit stark, isn't it?

IRVING: What?

FRANKIE: It's not my cup of tea.

IRVING: Yeh, well – it's masculine.

FRANKIE: Mm . . . could do with a woman's touch, couldn't it?

IRVING: Yeh, well, there's no shortage of that around here, is there, eh? Hey, Vernon!

　　[*Vernon enters, wearing a naughty apron.*]

VERNON: What's that, Irving?

IRVING: I say – there's no shortage of the woman's touch around here, is there, eh? [*He laughs uproariously.*]

　　[*Frankie exits to the kitchen.*]

VERNON: No, no; no shortage of that.

IRVING: Oh, I like your pinny.

VERNON: Oh, yes. Yes. Well, it does the job.

IRVING: Keeps the splashes off, eh?

[*Vernon picks up the wine Irving has brought.*]

VERNON: Oh, yes ... yes, I've seen this one in the supermarket.

IRVING: It's supposed to be quite good.

VERNON: Mm ... it's always worth taking a risk, isn't it?

FRANKIE [*off*]: Oh, Christ!

VERNON: What's wrong now, Frankie?

[*Frankie enters.*]

FRANKIE: Have you smelt your steak, Ver?

VERNON: No, Frankie, I haven't smelt my steak. I was under the impression it was still in the packet.

FRANKIE: Well, just go and give it a sniff.

VERNON: What's wrong with it?

FRANKIE: Just go and smell it.

VERNON: All right.

[*Vernon exits to the kitchen, followed by Irving.*]

FRANKIE: Jesus Christ! [*She sits on the sofa and eats some nuts.*]

[*Irving enters, much amused.*]

IRVING: Ooh, what a pong – eh?

[*He goes back to the kitchen.*]

  [*Off*] Aw! It's really horrible, isn't it?

[*Irving enters with one of the steaks in its packet.*]

  Look at it!

FRANKIE: Oh, take it away, for Christ's sake!

IRVING: Where d'you get it?

[*Vernon enters.*]

VERNON: In the supermarket.

FRANKIE: Fatal. *Never* buy steak in the supermarket, Ver. You should know that.

VERNON: Where d'you expect me to buy it?

FRANKIE: At the butcher's.

[*Vernon exits to the kitchen.*]

IRVING: Look!

FRANKIE: I don't want to look at it. Dear, oh, dear. I suppose they're all the same, are they?

[*Vernon enters with the other two steaks in their packets.*]

VERNON: 'Course they're all the same – I got them in the same bloody shop. Jesus Christ, I don't believe this, I don't bloody believe it.

FRANKIE: Well, you'll have to take them back.

VERNON: I'm going to report these bastards to the Area Health Authority, I'll take them to court! One mouthful of this garbage we could've all gone down with food-poisoning, could've bloody killed us. I'll sue these sods for every penny they've got, I'll get them closed down if it's the last thing I do. [*As he speaks, he takes a pocket calculator from his case.*] It's not as if you don't have to pay for it – it costs a bloody fortune – look at this: two pounds four pence; two pounds seven pence . . .

IRVING: One ninety-eight.

VERNON: God Almighty! Six pounds nine pence! You spend six pounds nine pence on best steak and what d'you wind up with? Putrified bloody horsemeat!

FRANKIE: Well, there's no point in getting in a state about it, Ver.
        [*During the following, Vernon goes and puts the steaks in the kitchen, and returns.*
        He sits at the table, gulping down some wine and a bit of his bread roll.]

VERNON: I'm going to take this in, Monday morning, and ram it down that bastard's throat. He won't know what's bloody hit him. I'll stuff it up his backside. I've had trouble with that sod before; sold me some rancid butter, didn't he?

IRVING: What, and you went back there?

VERNON: 'Course I went back there, Irving, there's nowhere else to go – all the other shops have closed down, you're left with bloody supermarkets!

IRVING: Oh, well, you've got to watch everything you buy these days.

FRANKIE: Yes, it's true – look at our wall-unit.

IRVING: Yeh – unbelievable.

FRANKIE: Disgusting.

IRVING: Had a great gouge out of the end!

FRANKIE: That's right – I said we should've gone to Brent Cross.

IRVING: That wouldn't have made any difference.

FRANKIE: And the hair-drier – look what happened to that.

IRVING: Nearly blew her ear off.

FRANKIE: Took it back to the shop, and they said, 'Where's the guarantee?'

IRVING: Turned into black melted plastic.

FRANKIE: And the washing-machine: that flooded the kitchen after a week, didn't it?

IRVING: I came home, and she was paddling!

FRANKIE: You don't need a guarantee, do you?

IRVING: No, not if you know your Consumers' Rights: I told them, it's the retailer's responsibility to ensure that goods are of merchantable quality.

FRANKIE: That's right!

VERNON: I'll give this bloody retailer 'merchantable quality'! Right: get your coats on. We're going out.

> [*Vernon puts his apron over the back of one of the dining-chairs, and exits to his bedroom.*]

IRVING: Where are we going?

VERNON [*off*]: I'm taking you out for a meal.

IRVING: Oh, that's good, isn't it?

> [*Frankie picks up the apron, and exits to the kitchen.*]

IRVING: What are you doing?

FRANKIE [*off*]: Nothing!

IRVING: Eh?

> [*Vernon enters, wearing a bomber jacket.*]

VERNON: Are you ready?

IRVING: Oh, yes. Ready and willing. Where are you taking us?

VERNON: Schooner. [*He switches off the music centre.*]

IRVING: Oh, great. Which one?

VERNON: Wembley. [*He switches off the lamp on the bar.*]

IRVING: Hendon one's good.

VERNON: We're going to Wembley. [*He switches off the lamp on the wall-unit.*]

IRVING: Hendon's nearer, though.

VERNON: We're going to Wembley, Irving.

> [*Frankie enters, wearing Vernon's apron, and with a kitchen knife in one hand and an unpeeled raw onion in the other.*]

FRANKIE: Have you got any mixed herbs, Ver?

VERNON: Christ almighty, Frankie – what are you playing at?

IRVING: What are you doing?

FRANKIE: I'm just going to whip something up – it won't take me five minutes.

IRVING: Vernon's taking us out for a meal.

FRANKIE: Well, there's no need, is there? Sit down, relax, enjoy yourselves. I'll be back in a moment.

> [*Frankie exits to the kitchen.*
> *Irving and Vernon follow her into the hall.*]

VERNON: There's nothing in the kitchen, Frankie!

FRANKIE [*off*]: I'm going to make a vegetable gratin.

VERNON [*returning to the lounge*]: I don't want vegetables, *I want meat*! God almighty!

> [*Frankie returns. She takes off the apron, and replaces it on the chair.*]

FRANKIE: All right, please yourself. I was only trying to help.

[*Vernon exits to get Frankie's coat.*]

IRVING: What's the matter with you? It's a free meal!

FRANKIE: Irving!

IRVING: Shall we follow in our car?

[*Vernon enters with Frankie's coat.*]

VERNON: We'll take my car.

IRVING: Oh, right. That'll save petrol.

[*Irving finishes his glass of wine, whilst Vernon helps Frankie on with her coat, touching her body momentarily as he does so. This is not seen by Irving.*]

VERNON: Right. I'm sorry about all this. It's a total disaster, and I'm deeply, deeply ashamed.

FRANKIE: Well, there's no need to apologize, Ver.

VERNON: There's every need to apologize, Frankie.

FRANKIE: Well, come along, let's go if we're going; I'm starving.

[*During the following, they all leave the flat, Vernon putting out lights and closing doors as they go.*]

IRVING: Which way are we going?

VERNON: Underpass.

IRVING: Neasden?

VERNON: Of course bloody Neasden!

IRVING: No, no, no – you want to cut through to the Harrow Road.

VERNON: Don't be stupid, Irving.

IRVING [*off*]: That brings you right out into Wembley Central.

VERNON [*off*]: I know the way, Irving.

IRVING [*off*]: You want the Broadway, don't you?

VERNON [*off*]: I'll do it my way, Irving.

[*They have gone. The lights fade quickly to a Blackout.*]

SCENE 3

The same. Later that evening.
The room is as Vernon and the others left it.

JACKIE [*off, hardly audible*]: D'you wanna go through? All right? Just go through.

[*The hall light is switched on.*]

[*Off, more audibly*] Ooh, it's all dark.

[*Jackie enters, wearing a fur jacket and carrying her handbag and a bottle of whisky. She puts on the main light.*
Muhammad enters.]

What's going on? [*She puts the bottle on the table.*] Had some friends over.
   [*Muhammad leans against the wall, Jackie puts on the lamp on the wall-unit and goes into the hall.*
   She exits towards Vernon's room.]
[*Off*] Vernon! [*She knocks on Vernon's door.*] Vernon.
   [*Muhammad sits at the table.*
   Jackie comes back into the room, takes off her jacket and puts it on the sofa.]
You all right?

MUHAMMAD: In car; in taxi; in, er ...

JACKIE: Mm. Got a bit car-sick?

MUHAMMAD: Er ... [*He gestures above his head, meaning 'aeroplane'.*]

JACKIE: Yeh, 't's really smoky.

MUHAMMAD: Er ... no good.
   [*Jackie goes to the bar and switches on the lamp there.*]

JACKIE: D'you want a whisky? Whisky?

MUHAMMAD: La.[1]
   [*Jackie pours herself a whisky-and-water.*]

JACKIE [*indicating the sofa*]: D'you want to come and sit over here? It's nice and comfortable. Come and sit over here.

MUHAMMAD: I come?

JACKIE: Yeh.
   [*Muhammad crosses slowly to the sofa. He coughs once on the way.*]

MUHAMMAD [*as he crosses*]: Ismāh-ly.[2]

JACKIE: Mm. Yeh. You sure you don't want a whisky?

MUHAMMAD: La.

JACKIE: D'you want a glass of water? A glass of water?

MUHAMMAD: Water.

JACKIE [*going to the bar*]: Yeh, all right. I'll get you some. 'T's best thing, you know, if you're feeling a bit sick. Flush your system out. I hope Vernon gets back soon. 'T's my flatmate. [*She hands him a glass of water.*] Here y'are. 'E 'asn't really met any of my friends. Be good when 'e comes back and sees you'ere. That'll give 'im a shock. I bet 'e's never met an oil sheikh before. [*She lights a cigarette.*] D'you want a cigarette? Cigarette?

MUHAMMAD: Okay.
   [*Jackie gives him a cigarette and lights it for him.*]

JACKIE: All right? [*She sits down.*]
   [*Pause.*]

MUHAMMAD: Where this?

JACKIE: What?

MUHAMMAD: Where ... this?

JACKIE: Here? This is my flat, yeh? 'T's where I live.

MUHAMMAD: No London?

JACKIE: Yeh, it's London. 'T's Dollis Hill.

MUHAMMAD: Big, big.

JACKIE: Oh, yeh, it's two-bedroomed, you know.
    [*Muhammad finishes the water.*]
    D'you want another one?
    [*Muhammad does not understand.*]
    D'you want some more water?
    [*Muhammad makes a vague, affirmative gesture.*]
    Yeh, all right, I'll get you some.
    [*Jackie goes to the bar, and pours the water. Muhammad stubs out the
    cigarette in an ashtray.*]

MUHAMMAD: Excuse. [*He coughs.*]

JACKIE: Here you are. I'll stick it down here, all right? [*She puts the glass
    on the floor beside him.*]

MUHAMMAD: Ismāh-ly.[3] Make, er ... Where?

JACKIE: What?

MUHAMMAD: Water.

JACKIE: It's down there, yeh? It's on the floor.

MUHAMMAD: Okay. [*He picks it up slowly.*]
    [*Pause.*]

JACKIE: 'Ow long you been over here?

MUHAMMAD: Excuse?

JACKIE: 'Ow long 'ave you been in London?

MUHAMMAD: London, big, big.

JACKIE: Yeh. You over 'ere on business?

MUHAMMAD: Business, business.

JACKIE: What sort of business you doing over 'ere? Is it deals with BP
    and that, yeh?

MUHAMMAD: Business ma'a[4] Abdullah.

JACKIE: Oh, you do business with Abdullah?

MUHAMMAD: Business ma'a Abdullah.

JACKIE: Yeh.

MUHAMMAD: Wa[5] Ibrahim; you know?

JACKIE: Yeh ...

MUHAMMAD: Wa Marwan. You know him?

JACKIE: Yeh ... No. No, I know Abdullah. Abdullah is a very old friend
    of mine. I have known him for a year.

MUHAMMAD: Abdullah come here?

JACKIE: No, he's not coming here.

    [*Pause.*]

MUHAMMAD: Where girl?

JACKIE: What?

MUHAMMAD: Where, er ... Albanāt hadoleech?[6]

JACKIE: I don't understand.

MUHAMMAD: Where girl? Where? Is er – you, is girl, girl, girl, girl, girl.

JACKIE: Oh girls, yeh? No, I told you, I don't share with girls. I share with a gentleman friend of mine, Vernon. We're just good friends.

MUHAMMAD: No, friend. Marwan, he my brother.

JACKIE: Oh, really?

MUHAMMAD: Ibrahim, he my, mm, family ...

JACKIE: Yeh.

MUHAMMAD: Er ... business.

JACKIE: Oh, it's family business, yeh?

MUHAMMAD: Business.

JACKIE: Oh, it's good, you know. Means you can trust people. No one's gonna do you.

MUHAMMAD: Important.

JACKIE: Is it very big deals, yeh?

MUHAMMAD: London.

JACKIE: Yeh, I really want Vernon to meet you, you know. D'you meet a lot of other millionaires and tycoons and that?

    [*Muhammad does not understand.*]

    What sort of business are you setting up in London? Is it very big oil deals?

MUHAMMAD: Sheriket es-Sālim.[7]

    [*Pause.*]

JACKIE: Yeh.

    [*Pause.*]

    Cheers!

MUHAMMAD: Excuse?

JACKIE: Cheers.

MUHAMMAD: Cheers?

JACKIE: Yeh.

MUHAMMAD [*patting the sofa*]: Is good!

JACKIE: What?

MUHAMMAD: Is good.

JACKIE: Oh, yeh, it's lovely – it's nice and comfortable.

MUHAMMAD: In my country, many, many English cheers.

JACKIE: Oh, really? D'you buy a lot of them over there?

MUHAMMAD: Is, er – Arads.

JACKIE: Arabs?

MUHAMMAD: Arads.

JACKIE: I don't understand.

MUHAMMAD: Is Arads' cheers. Is, er, Arads, is shop, Arads.

JACKIE: 'Arrods!

MUHAMMAD: Arads.

JACKIE: Oh, yeh, that's nice. D'you shop there?

MUHAMMAD: Is shop.

JACKIE: 'T's a nice shop, you know – it's very classy.

MUHAMMAD: Is shop.

JACKIE: I buy my make-up there, you know, perfume and that.

MUHAMMAD: Is shop.

JACKIE: Yeh.

   [*Pause.*]

  Is your brother in the hotel with you?

MUHAMMAD: Excuse?

JACKIE: Is your brother staying with you, in the hotel?

MUHAMMAD: Hotel Royal Garden.

JACKIE: Oh, really . . . ? Yeh, it's a nice hotel, you know? I have been
   there.

MUHAMMAD: You, er – la.[8]

JACKIE: What?

MUHAMMAD: You, er – no.

JACKIE: Look, I'm telling you: I've been there.

MUHAMMAD: La. Er, manty fāh'ma.[9]

JACKIE: Look: I have been to the Royal Garden Hotel. For drinks,
   y'know? Cocktails, actually.

MUHAMMAD: You English?

JACKIE: Yeh.

MUHAMMAD: No American?

JACKIE: No.

MUHAMMAD: Okay.

   [*Pause.*]

  [*Pointing at the television*] Video?

JACKIE: No, it's a television.

MUHAMMAD: Television ma'a[10] video?

JACKIE: No.

MUHAMMAD: Okay.

   [*Pause.*]

  What your name?

JACKIE: Jackie.

MUHAMMAD: Excuse?

JACKIE: Jackie, yeh?

MUHAMMAD: Jackie-yeh.

JACKIE: No. Jackie. Like Jackie Kennedy, you know? Onassis?

MUHAMMAD [*none the wiser*]: Okay.

　　[*Pause. Jackie goes to the bar.*]

JACKIE: D'you want a drink yet? Yeh? D'you want a whisky? Whisky?

MUHAMMAD: Whisky.

JACKIE: Yeh, all right.

MUHAMMAD: Oh, is, er ...

JACKIE: What's the matter?

MUHAMMAD: Is, er ...

JACKIE: This? 'T's a bar, yeh? It's nice. Not many people have got one
　　of these.

MUHAMMAD [*getting up*]: Okay. [*He goes to the bar, where he takes out a
　　thick wad of money.*] Hādha bkem?[11]

JACKIE: What?

MUHAMMAD: Er, er, take, er, take ...

JACKIE: What's that for? You don't have to pay for it. No! [*She walks
　　away from the bar.*]

　　[*Muhammad is puzzled, and puts the money away.*]

　My friend'll probably be back soon.

MUHAMMAD: Excuse?

JACKIE: My friend, will be back soon. Soon.

MUHAMMAD: Soon?

JACKIE: Yeh.

MUHAMMAD: Inshallah.[12] [*He gulps down his whisky quickly, in one go.*] Er
　　... where ... hammām?[13]

JACKIE: What?

MUHAMMAD: Where, er, where ...

JACKIE: 'T's the matter? D'you want the toilet? Toilet?

MUHAMMAD: Toilet, okay.

JACKIE: Yeh, all right, I'll show you.

　　[*She takes him out into the hall.*]

　Will you come round? Come through, yeh? 'T's down there. Right
　down that way. No, go on straight down the bottom. That's it. Yeh.
　[*She comes back into the room.*]

　　[*Pause.*]

MUHAMMAD [*coming back into the room*]: Excuse. Er ... ibreeg,[14] er ...
　　water ... make ...

JACKIE: D'you want the bathroom? Bathroom?

MUHAMMAD: Make . . .

JACKIE: Yeh, it's round there, through that door round there.

MUHAMMAD: Okay.

JACKIE: All right.

> [*Muhammad goes out of one door and back in through the other. Jackie goes into the hall and points towards the bathroom. Muhammad follows her.*]

No, not there, look, round here, yeh, next to the toilet? That one, yeh. That's it. [*She comes back into the room.*]

MUHAMMAD [*following her*]: Excuse . . . em – ibreeg.[14]

JACKIE: Don't understand.

MUHAMMAD: Ibreeg . . . wallah[15] . . . make, er . . . water. Make, er . . .

JACKIE: D'you want a glass of water, yeh? A glass of water? [*She points to the water-jug.*]

> [*Muhammad attempts to pick up the jug. She takes it.*]

'T's all right, I'll pour it out for you. [*She pours him a glass of water, and holds it out to him.*]

> [*Muhammad takes the jug, and goes out of the room with it.*]

[*Following him*] What's the matter? No, you don't want that. Can I have that back, please? Where are you taking that?

> [*Muhammad exits to the toilet with the jug.*
>
> *Jackie pauses for a moment, then goes back into the lounge, perplexed. She puts on the record left on the turntable by Vernon, then sits down. Pause. The toilet flushes, off. She regains her composure.*
>
> *Muhammad enters.*]

Are you all right?

MUHAMMAD: Okay.

JACKIE: What 'ave you done with the jug?

MUHAMMAD: Okay.

JACKIE: What, have you done, with the water-jug?

MUHAMMAD: Okay.

JACKIE [*getting up*]: Jesus! What's 'e done with it?

> [*Jackie rushes past Muhammad, and exits to the toilet.*]

MUHAMMAD [*following her into the hall*]: I come now?

> [*Once out of the room, Muhammad goes the other way, not having seen which way Jackie went.*]

[*Off*] Where he go? Excuse. Excuse. [*He knocks on Jackie's bedroom door.*]

> [*Jackie enters with the jug. She almost smells inside it, but doesn't quite. She shudders. She puts it back on the bar. She is disgusted. Muhammad enters.*]

Okay. Excuse. Is many, many, er, make, er ...

JACKIE: Look, when we was in the pub, did Abdullah explain to you
why you was comin' 'ere?

MUHAMMAD: Excuse?

JACKIE: Did Abdullah explain to you, *you*, why *you* was comin' 'ere? *Here*.
[*She points downwards, to the ground, as it were; but she happens to be
standing over the sofa, and Muhammad therefore takes 'Here' to
refer specifically to the sofa.*]

MUHAMMAD: Here?

JACKIE: Yeh.

MUHAMMAD: Okay, understand. Excuse!
[*Muhammad crosses to the sofa. Jackie moves away from it.*]

JACKIE: Just better to be straight, you know?

MUHAMMAD [*indicating the sofa*]: Here?

JACKIE: Yeh.
[*Muhammad gestures to indicate that Jackie should remove the ashtray
and the dish of nuts from the sofa.*]

MUHAMMAD: Okay, er, make, er ...
[*Jackie does nothing.*]
Okay, ana asawweeha![16] [*He puts the things on the side-table, muttering*]
Ēsh hal warta! Ēsh hal warta! ala kull hāl[17] ...

JACKIE: What's the matter? You all right?
[*He stands, waiting for her to sit with him on the sofa. He gestures to that
effect. Pause. She does not join him. Eventually, he sits down. Pause.*]
Got a car in London?

MUHAMMAD: Excuse?

JACKIE: Do you drive a car?

MUHAMMAD: Car ...

JACKIE: Yeh! In London.

MUHAMMAD: Taxi, no good. [*He indicates his stomach.*]

JACKIE: Oh, yeh, no, no, I mean – have you got a car? In your country ...

MUHAMMAD: In my country ...

JACKIE: Do you drive a car?

MUHAMMAD: Car? Many, many.

JACKIE: Oh, really?

MUHAMMAD: In my country is er, Pontiac, is Cadillac, is Toyota, is
Datsun, is Mercedes, is Rolls-Royce.

JACKIE: You got a Rolls-Royce, yeh?

MUHAMMAD: Many, many.

JACKIE [*miming driving*]: You got a chauffeur? You got a *chauffeur*?

MUHAMMAD: You? La.[18]

JACKIE: What?

MUHAMMAD: You – er, no.

JACKIE: Yeh, I drive.

MUHAMMAD: La!

JACKIE: I do. I've got a driving licence.

MUHAMMAD: In my country, is, er, mm ... [*indicating himself*] make, er, car: er ... girl, la.

JACKIE: Don't girls drive?
    [*Muhammad tuts.*]
    Why not?

MUHAMMAD [*tutting*]: Hādha suāl mustaheel.[19]
    [*Long pause.*]

JACKIE: D'you want a cigarette?

MUHAMMAD: Okay.
    [*While Jackie is lighting his cigarette, Muhammad holds her wrist.*]

JACKIE: No, 't's all right. What sort of places have you been to in London?

MUHAMMAD: Excuse?

JACKIE: Been to any clubs? Clubs.

MUHAMMAD: Club! I go club.

JACKIE: Oh. There's a lot of nice clubs in London. I'll tell you what: we'll go to a nice club next week, yeh? Have a nice meal, you know? Steak an' champagne an' that, yeh?

MUHAMMAD: Excuse?

JACKIE: You and me. YOU, will take ME.

MUHAMMAD: Now?

JACKIE: No, not now, no. Next week, yeh?

MUHAMMAD: Okay. Inshallah.[20]
    [*Pause.*]
    What him?

JACKIE: What?

MUHAMMAD: What him?

JACKIE: This? 'T's my brooch, yeh? Brooch? 'T's nice, yeh. D'you like it?

MUHAMMAD: What him?

JACKIE: It's cherries. Cherries, what you eat?

MUHAMMAD: You eat him?

JACKIE: Yeh. 'T's nice. D'you wanna 'ave a look?

MUHAMMAD: Ajeeb[21] ...

JACKIE: All right, I'll show you. [*She takes off the brooch.*] There you are. 'S pretty, yeh? Pretty? [*She gives it to him.*] D'you like it?

MUHAMMAD: Shukran.[22]

JACKIE: Yeh, it's nice.

MUHAMMAD: Eat him. [*He puts the brooch in his mouth.*]

JACKIE: No, you don't eat 'em. No, they're not real, just pretend, you know.

MUHAMMAD: Okay. Shukran.[22] [*He puts it in his pocket.*]

JACKIE: I'm not giving them to you. 'T's not a present. [*After a pause*] Can I have my brooch back, please?

MUHAMMAD: Ajeeb![23]

JACKIE: Come on. Yeh?

MUHAMMAD: Okay.

JACKIE: All right – come on.
[*He gets up. He pulls out the wad of money, and offers it to her.*]
What's that? I don't want that, I want my brooch back, yeh, I don't want – I want my brooch.

MUHAMMAD: Hādha bkem?[24]

JACKIE: In your pocket.

MUHAMMAD: Na'am. Hādha bkem?[25]

JACKIE: My brooch. Yeh? Yeh.
[*He gets out the brooch. She snatches it from his hand.*]
Thank you. I don't want that. [*She puts on the brooch, using one of the mirrors on the wall.*]

MUHAMMAD: Oh, er, excuse.

JACKIE: Yeh.

MUHAMMAD: Understand. Is, er ... you make ... mm; I make – mm; al floos[26] is ... make, excuse. [*He sits down. He is extremely angry with himself. He tuts.*] H'maar akmar! Kaif irtakabt mithil hal-khata? Ismāh-ly.[27] Excuse.

JACKIE: Yeh, all right. [*She sits down.*]
[*Muhammad takes out a tube of Refreshers, a tube of Fruit Gums, and some worry-beads. He offers her a sweet.*]

MUHAMMAD: Okay?

JACKIE: What's that? Fruit Gums? No, I don't want one.
[*He puts a Refresher in his mouth, and puts the sweets and worry-beads away. Pause. Then he flicks cigarette ash on the floor.*]
D'you want an ashtray, yeh? [*She gets him an ashtray, and goes to the bar.*] Use an ashtray, don't flick ash on the carpet, you know, it's a nice rug. D'you want one? D'you want a whisky?

MUHAMMAD: Okay.
[*Jackie pours out the whiskies, just stopping herself from using the the jug. She uses the soda-syphon instead.*]

JACKIE [*looking at her watch*]: 'Ere y'are. All right? Yeh, Vernon'll be back
    soon. 'E's 'ad some friends over tonight for a party. Yeh, 'e's probably
    taken them on to a club, you know, they've gone dancing. Dancing.

MUHAMMAD: Dance?

JACKIE: Yeh.

MUHAMMAD: You dance?

JACKIE: What?

MUHAMMAD: Er, dance?

JACKIE: D'you wanna dance?

MUHAMMAD: Dance?

JACKIE: Yeh, all right.

MUHAMMAD: Okay?

JACKIE: Yeh.

MUHAMMAD: Okay. [*He settles back comfortably.*] Mumtāz!28

JACKIE: What's the matter?

MUHAMMAD: Make, akthar.29

JACKIE: Well, come on, you dance an' all, yeh?

MUHAMMAD: U ba'ad?30

JACKIE: No, I'm not dancing on my own!

MUHAMMAD: Make, urugsi!31

JACKIE: No, I feel stupid. [*She sits down.*]

MUHAMMAD: Make, er ...

JACKIE: Look, I'll dance with you, you know? I don't want to dance on
    me own.

MUHAMMAD: Okay, er ... [*He takes out the money.*] Okay?

JACKIE: What's that?

MUHAMMAD: Urugseely!32

JACKIE: What?

MUHAMMAD: Urugsi!33 [*He proceeds to peel off notes, one by one on to the sofa.*]

JACKIE: What's that for, yeh?

MUHAMMAD [*peeling off another note*]: Dance? [*Another.*] Dance?

JACKIE: Yeh, look – I'll dance with you!

MUHAMMAD [*another note*]: Dance?

JACKIE: I don't understand.

MUHAMMAD: Understand! [*Another note.*] Understand.

JACKIE: No, I don't.

MUHAMMAD: Okay, more. More; more? More; more; more. [*He continues
    to peel off notes.*]

JACKIE: Is that a present, yeh?

MUHAMMAD: More?

JACKIE: Are you giving that to me?

MUHAMMAD: Okay? Okay. [*He throws all the peeled-off notes on the floor.*]
Urugsi.[33]

JACKIE: I'll take it!

MUHAMMAD: Take, er, make, urugsi ...

JACKIE: I'm gonna take it, you know?

MUHAMMAD: Take. Take, take!

JACKIE: What, is it a present, yeh?

MUHAMMAD: Urugsi, urugsi.

JACKIE: I'm gonna take it.

MUHAMMAD: Take, take, take, take.

JACKIE: All right. [*She picks it all up.*] I've taken it.

MUHAMMAD: Okay, make, er ... dance.

JACKIE: I'll dance with you!

MUHAMMAD: More?

JACKIE: No.

MUHAMMAD: More!

JACKIE: No!

[*He starts throwing more notes across the floor.*]
What's that? I'm not picking it up down there.

MUHAMMAD: More?

JACKIE: No.

MUHAMMAD: More? More ...

JACKIE: I'll dance with you, you know? We'll dance together –

MUHAMMAD: More?

JACKIE: – all right?

MUHAMMAD: Okay?

JACKIE: Yeh.

MUHAMMAD: Okay.

JACKIE: Right. Come on, then. Come on. [*She gets up, and takes his hand.*]
[*He gets up.*]
That's it.

MUHAMMAD: Okay, now?

JACKIE: Yeh.

MUHAMMAD: Okay. [*He pushes her down on to the sofa.*]

JACKIE: What's the matter?

MUHAMMAD: Okay, make, er – el-treek;[34] okay, em ... [*He puts out the main light.*]

JACKIE: What're you doing?

MUHAMMAD: Okay, okay, make, er make ...

JACKIE [*getting up*]: No, look, leave the lights on, yeh?

MUHAMMAD: Okay ...

JACKIE: Look, Vernon'll be back soon, yeh?

MUHAMMAD [*grabbing her*]: Okay.

JACKIE: Will you stop pushing me?

[*He pushes her back on to the sofa.*]

What's the matter with you?

MUHAMMAD: Tsallakhy³⁵ ...

JACKIE [*getting up*]: Right. I'm gonna turn the lights on.

MUHAMMAD: La – khalleeha el-treek.³⁶

JACKIE: Look: you leave the lights on, d'you understand? On. All right?

[*She switches on the main light.*]

MUHAMMAD ⎫ [*together*]: La ... make, em.
JACKIE ⎭   No, you don't touch them, you know? D'you understand?

MUHAMMAD: Okay. Mā dām, you, el-treek.³⁷ Understand.

JACKIE: Right?

MUHAMMAD: Okay, okay.

JACKIE: Yeh. You don't touch them, yeh?

MUHAMMAD: Okay, make, er ...

JACKIE: Yeh.

MUHAMMAD: Okay ... [*He pats the sofa for her to join him.*] Okay.

JACKIE: Yeh, all right. You leave them alone. [*She sits with him.*] It's just that my friend'll be back soon.

MUHAMMAD: Soon?

JACKIE: Yeh.

MUHAMMAD: Inshallah.³⁸ [*He settles back resignedly.*]

[*Pause.*]

JACKIE: Did you buy any clothes when you went to Oxford Street?

MUHAMMAD: Excuse?

JACKIE: When you went to Oxford Street, yeh? Did you buy any clothes? Clothes. [*She demonstrates by touching his jacket.*]

MUHAMMAD: Clothes!

JACKIE: Yeh, d'you understand?

MUHAMMAD: Clothes! Okay! Understand! Clothes: it mean 'Hadoum'. [*He stands up, and removes his jacket.*] Make, el-treek,³⁹ mm, okay ... [*He starts turning out the lights again. Jackie follows him, turning them back on.*]

JACKIE: No, look, I've told you, you leave the lights on, yeh? Listen: when we was in the pub, Abdullah told you you was just comin' back with me to meet a few friends of mine, and 'ave some nice drinks, you know?

MUHAMMAD: Okay. Khallās.[40] [*He picks up the whole telephone, and holds out the receiver to Jackie.*] Okay. Er ... make him Abdullah.

JACKIE: I don't know his number.

MUHAMMAD: Make him Abdullah.

JACKIE: I don't know his phone number.

MUHAMMAD: No?

JACKIE: No.

MUHAMMAD: Okay. [*He puts back the telephone.*]
　　[*Pause.*]
　　[*Muttering*] Ēsh hal warta[41] ... Okay.
　　[*He attempts to take back the money, which Jackie is still holding.*]

JACKIE: No. No, you gave it to me, yeh? – it's a present. A deal's a deal, you know? – you don't make an agreement, and then back out of it.

MUHAMMAD: Okay, dance?

JACKIE: Yeh, I'll dance with *you*!

MUHAMMAD: Dance?

JACKIE: Yeh.

MUHAMMAD: Il humdillah,[42] okay! Okay, make er, make er, dance, okay?

JACKIE: Come on, then, come on. You come and dance an' all, you know?

MUHAMMAD: Mumtāz! Okay, akthar![43] [*He sits at the table.*]

JACKIE: I'm not dancing on me own, yeh?

MUHAMMAD: Okay, urugsi, urugseely, make, er make – okay, make, er dance, make, er okay, take er, okay, tsallakhy! Tayyib! Okay! Urugsi! Urugseely! Hadoum!![44] [*He opens the whisky left on the table by Jackie. He looks for a clean glass on the table, smelling them.*]

JACKIE: What's the matter, d'you want your glass, yeh? Here you are, here's your glass, all right?

MUHAMMAD: Okay, you er ... [*He pulls her on to his knee.*]

JACKIE [*friendly*]: What're you doing?

MUHAMMAD: Okay, tsallakhy![45] [*He pulls at her clothes.*]

JACKIE [*jumping off*]: No, leave that. Look, we don't pull people's clothes, you know? Gentlemen don't do that in England!

MUHAMMAD: Er, make belly ...

JACKIE: What?

MUHAMMAD: Make belly-dance.

JACKIE: Ballet? I don't do ballet!

MUHAMMAD: Make him, make er, okay, mumtāz![46]
　　[*He pats her bottom. She revolves.*]

JACKIE: What're you doing, yeh?

MUHAMMAD: Okay, akthar, make, er – mumtāz!⁴⁷

JACKIE: No, I can't keep turning round in circles!
  [*She is turning round in circles. He continues to pat her bottom.*]

MUHAMMAD: Okay. Akthar!⁴⁸

JACKIE [*not unfriendly*]: What you doin', yeh? Don't be stupid.
  [*Frankie enters.*]
  Oh, hi.
  [*Muhammad seizes Frankie's arm.*]

MUHAMMAD: Okay, two?

FRANKIE: Hey! D'you mind?
  [*Frankie runs out.*]

JACKIE: No, it's all right, yeh – [*she starts to pursue Frankie*] – no, no, it's
  all right! [*She remembers the money on the floor and rushes back to pick it all
  up.*]
  [*The following line runs simultaneously with the preceding line, starting after
  Frankie's exit.*]

FRANKIE [*off*]: Vernon! There's a bloke in there tried to grab hold of
  my arm!

MUHAMMAD [*to Jackie*]: Is okay, is, er, more . . .
  [*Vernon, Frankie and Irving enter.*]

VERNON: What's going on?

JACKIE: Oh, hi, Ver.

VERNON: Who's this?

JACKIE: No, it's all right, 'e's a friend of mine.

VERNON: Strange sort of friend – she says he just grabbed her arm.

FRANKIE: That's right.

JACKIE: Oh, no. No, 'e was just tryin' to give 'er a drink, you know?

FRANKIE: Well, it's a queer way of going about it.

JACKIE: Yeh, well, 'e don't understand. I think she was a bit funny with
  'im.

FRANKIE: Look: he grabbed hold of my coat!

JACKIE: No, 'e didn't.

FRANKIE: 'E did!

VERNON: All right, Frankie!

IRVING: Have you been molesting my wife?

VERNON: Irving!

FRANKIE: This isn't Jackie, is it?

VERNON: Of course it's Jackie! Jackie Scragg, Frankie Gammon. Irving
  Gammon.

IRVING: Evening.

JACKIE: Hi.

FRANKIE: Jesus Christ!

[*Frankie exits to hang up her coat.*
Jackie discreetly stuffs the money in her bag.]

MUHAMMAD: Okay? Okay. [*To Vernon*] You go. [*To Irving*] You go.

IRVING: What!

VERNON: Jackie, who is this character?

[*Frankie enters.*]

JACKIE: It's all right, Vern, yeh? Vernon: I'd like you to meet a friend
of mine. Mohammed. [*This is how she pronounces his name.*] He's in
London, doing some very important big business deals.

VERNON: Mohammed?

JACKIE: Yeh.

VERNON: Jesus Christ! *A bloody Arab!!!*

BLACKOUT

ACT II

The same. A few minutes later.
   The light in the kitchen is now on. Frankie is sitting on a bar-stool. Irving is lurking about. Muhammad and Jackie are standing together.

JACKIE: What's the matter? Your tie? It's all right. [*She adjusts his tie.*]
   That's it. All right?
MUHAMMAD: Okay. Soon? Soon?
FRANKIE: Soon he'll be all right.
JACKIE: D'you want to come and sit down, yeh? 'Ave a little whisky?
   Whisky? [*She sits down.*]
MUHAMMAD [*sitting down*]: La.⁴⁹
IRVING: No, they're not allowed to drink, you know. That's why they
   come over here.
      [*Vernon enters; he puts on the apron, and proceeds to clear the table.*]
FRANKIE: How do you know?
IRVING: Well, it's their religion, isn't it?
JACKIE: He does; he drinks whisky.
IRVING: Does he? Naughty boy! You'll get the cane!
FRANKIE: Stupid bugger!
JACKIE [*to Muhammad*]: No, it's all right, don't take any notice of him,
   yeh – he's joking. It's a joke.
VERNON: Was that a joke, Irving?
IRVING: No, I'm serious. They get their hands chopped off, as
   well.
FRANKIE: Irving!
JACKIE: No, they don't.
IRVING: They do; I've seen it on the telly.
      [*Pause.*]
   It's very nice to meet you . . . Jackie. I've heard a lot about you.
JACKIE: Oh, really?
      [*Vernon exits to the kitchen.*]
IRVING: Quite surprised to see you, really. I should've thought in your
   line, it was pretty well an all-night job.
JACKIE: Well, it is, yeh. I just finished early tonight.
IRVING: I should've thought Saturday was the big night?
JACKIE: Oh, yeh, it's very busy on Saturdays, lot of heavy action.
IRVING: Lot of people there, eh?

JACKIE: Oh, yeh, get a few punters in, y'know, sort of eleven-deep round the tables tonight, Manhattan skyline.

FRANKIE: Oh, yes?

IRVING: Lot of money flying about, eh?

JACKIE: Yeh, a few pennies to spend, you know?

IRVING [*leaning across Jackie to reach the ashtray*]: Excuse me.

JACKIE: 'T's all right.

[*Vernon enters with a tea-tray. He continues to clear the table.*]

VERNON: Where does this character spring from, Jackie? What's his country of origin?

JACKIE: He's an Arab, yeh? From Saudi Arabia.

FRANKIE: Oh, Arabia?

MUHAMMAD: Saudi Arabia.

JACKIE: It's your country.

MUHAMMAD: In my country.

FRANKIE: That's nice.

JACKIE: Yeh, 'e's over here settin' up oil deals 'an that.

VERNON: Oh, is he?

IRVING: They're really wealthy, aren't they?

JACKIE: Oh, yeh, they walk in the club and cash up a few grand without thinkin' about it, you know?

IRVING: Yeh, they go in for a lot of gambling.

JACKIE: Oh, yeh. Yeh, well, it's relaxation for 'em, innit? D'you go gamin'?

[*Vernon exits to the kitchen with the tray.*]

IRVING: How d'you mean? Oh, gaming? Yeh, well ... a bit – you know.

JACKIE: Yeh, you've got to 'ave the money to spend, 'aven't you?

IRVING: No, it's not that. Don't get the time. Don't get into the West End very much.

FRANKIE: What you talking about? 'Course we do.

IRVING: When?

FRANKIE: Saturday nights.

IRVING: Yes ... go and see a film occasionally.

JACKIE: What sort of clubs d'you go to, then?

IRVING: Um ...

[*Pause.*]

FRANKIE: Different ones.

[*Frankie exits to join Vernon in the kitchen.*]

IRVING: Forgotten, really, um ... been to a few with friends. Haven't been to yours, though.

JACKIE: 'T's a nice club, you know? There's a lot of big money goin' about.

IRVING: I shall have to come in and see you some time.

JACKIE: Yeh ... well, we're not allowed to talk to people when we're working, you know? They're very strict about that.

IRVING: No chance of a few free chips, then, eh?

JACKIE: Oh, no.

  [*Vernon enters, followed by Frankie.*]

VERNON: Who's this friend of his that you know, then, Jackie?

JACKIE: Oh, 'e's a very old friend of mine.

VERNON: Oh, yes? Who's that?

JACKIE: He's called Abdullah.

VERNON: Abdullah?

JACKIE: Mm.

VERNON: Jesus Christ! Another one!

MUHAMMAD: You know Abdullah?

VERNON: No, I don't know Abdullah!

  [*Vernon exits to the kitchen.*]

JACKIE: No, 'e don't know 'im, 'e's just a friend of mine.

MUHAMMAD [*to Frankie*]: You know Abdullah?

FRANKIE [*going towards the hall*]: Ooh, no, I don't know him either.

  [*Vernon enters.*]

VERNON [*as he enters*]: Get out the way, Frankie! [*He continues to clear the table.*]

MUHAMMAD [*to Irving*]: You know Abdullah?

IRVING: What?

JACKIE: No, 'e's just my friend, yeh?

IRVING: How long you been there, then?

JACKIE: What?

IRVING: In your present position, if you'll pardon the expression. [*He laughs uproariously.*]

JACKIE: Oh, just a few months – well, I'll probably sort of move on later in the year, you know, go and work abroad an' that.

FRANKIE: Oh, really?

JACKIE: Oh, yeh, if you're London-trained you can go anywhere in the world.

FRANKIE: Can you?

JACKIE: Yeh, I could go to Amsterdam, you know, you can pick up about five hundred a week over there.

FRANKIE: That's a lot of money, isn't it?

  [*Vernon has now completely cleared up. He exits to the kitchen.*]

JACKIE: Yeh, it is. I might go to Africa, an' all, you know. Nigeria – get a lot of big punters over there.

FRANKIE: You'll have to get inoculated.

[*Frankie exits to the kitchen.*]

JACKIE [*calling after her*]: Yeh, I know. I will.

[*During the following speech, Frankie discreetly returns and closes the dining-area door, then goes back to Vernon in the kitchen.*]

Might go to the States an' all, you know: Atlantic City's gone legal.

IRVING: Yeh, I thought it probably would.

JACKIE: Picked up forty million in the first week.

IRVING: Oh, easily, easily.

JACKIE: Quite a few of us go and work on the cruisers an' all, you know – I might go to Miami and the Bahamas an' that, go on the *QE2*, ah, it's everyone's dream to work on that boat, you know, it's lovely.

IRVING: You must lead a really exciting life.

JACKIE: Yeh – you meet a lot of people.

IRVING: Pity you can't talk to them – eh? [*He laughs uproariously.*]

JACKIE: Not really.

IRVING: Get to know them. [*He gets up, and looks through the open lounge door in the general direction of the kitchen.*]

JACKIE: Don't really want to, actually. To be quite honest, it don't pay to get too involved, you know; I know that don't sound very nice, but you can get it thrown back in your face.

MUHAMMAD: Okay, go?

IRVING: What?

MUHAMMAD: You, er, go?

IRVING: Go?

JACKIE [*to Muhammad*]: What, no, it's all right, he's just having a drink, yeh? [*To Irving*] D'you work with Vern, then?

IRVING: That's right. Yeh. [*He sits down.*]

JACKIE: Oh, really, how's it goin, you sellin'?

IRVING: Oh, yes, it's going really well, you know.

JACKIE: Yeh?

IRVING: We've had a lot of orders in recently, specially since the Metro came in.

JACKIE: 'T's right.

IRVING: It's aroused a lot of interest in Leyland in general.

MUHAMMAD: Excuse ...

IRVING: What?

JACKIE: Yeh, it's a nice little car, you know?

[*During the following, Muhammad gets up, and peers towards the kitchen through the clear window-pane in the closed door.*]

IRVING: It is, yeh; have you tried it?

JACKIE: No, I haven't, no.

IRVING: Oh, well, you'll have to come in for a test-drive, won't you?

JACKIE: Yeh . . . yeh, I might.

IRVING: Don't tell Vernon, though, eh?

JACKIE: Why not?

IRVING: Well, he might think I was poaching, mightn't he?

JACKIE: I don't see why.

[*Muhammad stands by the open door.*]

MUHAMMAD: Okay, go now.

IRVING: What?

MUHAMMAD: You make, er . . . go.

JACKIE: No, it's all right, he's just havin' a drink, yeh?

IRVING: Look, excuse me; I'm just having a chat with this young lady here.

JACKIE: Just come and sit down, have a nice little whisky, all right?

IRVING: It's funny you being brunette, you know; I thought you'd have red hair.

JACKIE: Oh, did you?

IRVING: Yeh.

MUHAMMAD: Here this, er, mm – girl. Is, er . . . here, is, er . . . barman ma'a[50] girl, make, er, like this. [*He claps together vertical cupped hands.*]

IRVING [*getting up*]: Eh?

MUHAMMAD: Is here, you make, er, em . . .

IRVING: I'm not going anywhere – right?

[*Irving exits to the kitchen.*
Muhammad closes the door behind him.]

MUHAMMAD: Okay.

JACKIE [*standing up*]: What's the matter? Come and sit down, yeh? Have a whisky. Whisky?

MUHAMMAD: Okay. [*He sits down in the centre of the sofa.*]

[*Jackie pours him a whisky.*
Frankie enters, a bit flustered, followed by Irving. She goes to her bag and adjusts her make-up.
Irving stands in the doorway, surveying the scene, then closes the door and exits to join Vernon in the kitchen.
Both doors are now closed. Muhammad is extremely confused.]

JACKIE [*giving the whisky to Muhammad*]: There you are. All right?

MUHAMMAD: La!

JACKIE: 'S the matter? I just got it for you.

> [*Loud mirth from the kitchen.*]

All right? I'll just stick it on 'ere, yeh? [*She puts the drink on the table.*] – you can 'elp yourself when you feel like it. [*She sits down beside him.*]

> [*Frankie finishes her make-up and moves across to the sofa.*]

FRANKIE: Quite nice-looking, really, isn't he?

JACKIE: Oh, yeh, well, they are, you know – get a lot of 'em in the club.

FRANKIE: Not too dark.

JACKIE: No. Well, they are quite dark, you know? It's a really hot country, where they live.

FRANKIE [*sitting on the other side of Muhammad*]: Yes, I know that.

> [*Pause.*]

Sweet little beard, isn't it?

JACKIE: Yeh, it's nice. I don't usually like beards, you know? – I don't like them when they're all over your face – that one's all right.

FRANKIE: Yes, it's neat, isn't it?

JACKIE: Yeh.

FRANKIE: Oh, hasn't he got nice eyes?

JACKIE: Yeh, lovely.

FRANKIE: Mm. Dark.

JACKIE: Mm.

FRANKIE: He's a bit like Omar Sharif, isn't he?

JACKIE: Yeh, he is, you know? I like him; he's really mysterious.

FRANKIE: Mind you, he's a bit overweight.

JACKIE: I don't know . . . I don't mind if it's spread out. Not like English blokes, drink beer all the time, pot bellies, it's 'orrible.

FRANKIE: Well, he's got a pot, hasn't he?

JACKIE: No, not really.

FRANKIE [*pointing*]: Well, what's that, then?

> [*Muhammad places his hands over his crutch.*]

Still, at least he hasn't got one of those things on.

JACKIE: What's that?

FRANKIE: You know – sheets.

JACKIE: Oh, no, they don't wear them; not when they're doing business, anyway: they wear really nice suits, you know – really expensive.

FRANKIE [*feeling Muhammad's lapel*]: Well, you can seen this is good quality, isn't it?

JACKIE [*feeling the other lapel*]: Yeh, it's lovely.

MUHAMMAD [*proceeding to remove his jacket*]: Okay.

JACKIE: No, it's all right! Have your drink, yeh? [*She hands him his glass.*] Whisky?

MUHAMMAD: Whisky, okay. [*He takes the glass.*]

JACKIE: Cheers.

FRANKIE: Cheers.

MUHAMMAD [*patting the sofa*]: Is good, cheers.

> [*Vernon and Irving enter through the lounge-area door and go to the bar. Muhammad immediately puts his whisky on Jackie's lap.*]

JACKIE: What's the matter?

VERNON: Everything goes wrong with your car, Irving.

IRVING: It's not my fault, is it?

VERNON: Of course it's your fault.

IRVING: It's the workshop, I mean, they don't check 'em up properly before they send 'em out.

VERNON: They check 'em out, it's you – it's the way you drive 'em, Irving.

IRVING: No, if they'd check 'em properly, they'd find out if it was a rogue car, wouldn't they?

VERNON: Not a rogue car, it's a rogue driver –

IRVING: Come on, Vernon, don't exaggerate. I mean, it's hardly my fault if the lock on the hatchback goes, is it?

VERNON: It's always something, Irving – all these little things, they mount up.

IRVING: It's like the carburettor. It's only going to be a fifteen-minute job, isn't it? Little twiddle with a screwdriver and it's done, eh?

VERNON: It's always you, though, isn't it?

JACKIE: Can I have the ashtray, Vernon?

> [*The following dialogue runs simultaneously with the preceding dialogue, and starts after Jackie's line 'What's the matter?'*]

FRANKIE: Would you pass the ashtray, please, Jackie?

JACKIE: Oh. All right. [*She passes it. Then, to Muhammad*] What's the matter?

> [*Muhammad says nothing.*]

FRANKIE: Could you pass the nuts over as well, please?

JACKIE [*passing them*]: D'you want some nuts, yeh? D'you want some peanuts?

FRANKIE: No; no, he doesn't.

JACKIE: I'll just get an ashtray, actually . . .

> [*She goes to the bar.*]

MUHAMMAD: I come now?

JACKIE: Can I have the ashtray, Vernon?

[*She takes it.*]

VERNON: D'you want a drink, Jackie?

JACKIE: No, it's all right, I've got one.

VERNON [*picking up the whisky bottle*]: Where did this come from, Jackie?

JACKIE: Oh, it's a really nice whisky, you know. Mohammed brought it.

VERNON: Did he?

JACKIE: Yeh.

VERNON: D'you want some, Mohammed? Whisky. Whisky?

MUHAMMAD: La.[51]

FRANKIE: Na. He doesn't, Ver.

JACKIE: Stick it down 'ere, all right? [*She puts down the ashtray.*]

IRVING: Stick it where you like, eh? [*He laughs uproariously.*]

VERNON: How about you, Frankie?

FRANKIE: Gin-and-tonic, please.

VERNON: Gin-and-tonic for the lady! [*He pours her a drink.*]

JACKIE: Here y'are; 'ere's your drink.

   [*Muhammad tuts.*]

  'T's the matter?

VERNON: Ice, Frankie?

FRANKIE: Please.

   [*Pause. Frankie utters her noise, q.v.*]

MUHAMMAD: Excuse?

FRANKIE: Eh?

   [*Pause. Muhammad takes some nuts from the dish in Frankie's lap.*]

VERNON: Here we are, Frankie. [*He hands her a drink.*]

FRANKIE: Thank you.

VERNON: Oh, glad to see you've got your appetite back.

FRANKIE: Mm ... just a bit.

IRVING: Yeh, well, she's not eaten for half an hour, has she, eh?

FRANKIE: There's no need to be rude, Irving.

VERNON: Don't listen to him, Frankie. Enjoy that cheesecake, did you?

FRANKIE: I did, thank you – it was a super meal, Vernon.

JACKIE: What d'you 'ave?

FRANKIE [*defensively*]: Steak ...

JACKIE: Oh, did you?

IRVING: Nice and juicy, mine was.

FRANKIE [*defensively*]: So was mine.

VERNON: They had T-bone steaks, these two.

JACKIE: Oh, really? I can never manage to get through one of them, you know?

VERNON: They had T-bone steaks with garnish; french fries, peas, grilled tomatoes ...

IRVING: Didn't have mushrooms, though, did they?

VERNON: No, they didn't have mushrooms, did they, Irving? But you do get mushrooms at the Berni, don't you?

IRVING: That's right, you do – hand-picked.

VERNON: Something else new I've learnt this evening ... Then they had prawn cocktails with roll-and-butter to start with. Then, seven different types of salad from the salad bar – there was coleslaw; potato salad; raisin; green salad; tomato salad; beetroot salad and bean salad; all with Thousand-Island Dressing; then there was cheesecake; and cheese-and-biscuits – three different kinds of cheese; coffee with cream, in a goblet; brandy; bottles of wine; not to mention the aperitifs to kick off with.

FRANKIE: Well, it's all-in, isn't it?

VERNON: It's not, as it happens – that's why I had the lamb-chops.

JACKIE: No, Mohammed was just saying, you know, he's going to take me out for a nice meal next week. We're gonna go to the Empress Club in Mayfair.

FRANKIE: Oh, that'll be nice for you.

JACKIE: Yeh, it's a nice club, you know – it's really smart.

VERNON: You'll enjoy that, won't you? Right up your street.

MUHAMMAD: Excuse?

VERNON [*making a drinking gesture*]: Have a little drinkie? Oh, lovely!

MUHAMMAD: Okay, I take orange juice.

JACKIE: Orange juice?

VERNON: You take orange juice? I'll get you an orange juice.

IRVING: I hope my wife's watching what she's drinking – I want to get home in one piece!

JACKIE: That's right, yeh.

FRANKIE: I know how much I can take.

IRVING: You're mixing them, aren't you? You've been on wine all evening.

FRANKIE: Look, you worry about yourself, and I'll worry about myself, all right?

IRVING: Well, who's driving, then, you or me?

FRANKIE: I don't mind – you can if you want to.

IRVING: Well, it's your car – you drive, right?

FRANKIE: All right, all right – don't go on about it.

IRVING: Right.

VERNON [*pouring orange juice*]: Does he want whisky in it? Do you want whisky in it, Abdullah? [*He adds whisky.*]

JACKIE: D'you want whisky, yeh? In your orange juice?

MUHAMMAD: Orange juice.

JACKIE: Yeh, yeh. All right. It's Mohammed, actually.

VERNON: Here you are, Smiler.

MUHAMMAD: Shukran.[52]

FRANKIE: Oh.

VERNON: Shookra? Is that what it is, Shookra? I like a drop of Shookra.

JACKIE: Is that what you call it, yah?

MUHAMMAD: Okay . . . [He takes out his wad of money.]

FRANKIE ⎫   Oh, Christ . . .
JACKIE ⎬ [together]: It's all right, you don't have to pay for it.
IRVING ⎭   Here, look at that.

VERNON: Got a few bob on him, hasn't he?

JACKIE: Yeh, 'e 'as, you know? [To Muhammad] You keep.

FRANKIE: It's free. Free.

VERNON: Does he want to pay me for it, does he?

JACKIE: No, don't be stupid.

MUHAMMAD: Okay, okay, make tip for barman.

VERNON: Does he think I'm the barman, does he, eh? I'm not proud, I'll take it – come on, come on.

IRVING: I should. Have it. Go on! He's got plenty to spare.

JACKIE: Stop it, yeh? It's probably what they do in his country. What sort of car 'ave you got?

IRVING: She's got a Clubman.

FRANKIE: Well, we've both got cars, haven't we?

IRVING: We run two cars!

FRANKIE: Oh, yes!

JACKIE: Mohammed's got a Rolls-Royce.

IRVING: Oh, yes.

FRANKIE: Oh. Rolls-Royce?

MUHAMMAD: Rolls-Royce. Many, many.

JACKIE: Yeh, 'e's got a lot of cars, you know?

FRANKIE: Has he?

MUHAMMAD: In my country. [He empties his glass, and holds it up.]

VERNON: Oh – here we go again! [Taking the glass] Yes, sir, coming up, sir, at your service, sir. [He goes to the bar and pours Muhammad another drink.]

JACKIE: He's got a Cadillac an' all, actually.

FRANKIE: Has he?

JACKIE: Yeh.

MUHAMMAD: English cars no good.

IRVING: What are you talking about? British cars are the best in the world, Rolls-Royce.

JACKIE: Well, 'e's got a Rolls, en' 'e?

IRVING: There you are.

JACKIE: No, they buy American cars, you know?

IRVING: Load of tin, they are.

JACKIE: They're nice and big, though, aren't they?

IRVING: Too big.

FRANKIE: No good in London.

JACKIE: Yes, but they like limousines, you know – plenty of room in the back.

IRVING: Put all their wives in, I should think, eh?

[Vernon approaches Muhammad with a tea-towel over one arm, and holding Muhammad's drink in the other hand.]

VERNON: Here, Irv, Irv! *[To Muhammad, servile mock-waiter]* Here you are, sir, your drink, sir, at your service, sir.

[Vernon and Irving laugh uproariously.]

MUHAMMAD *[taking the drink, oblivious to the joke]*: Elwāhid[53] go buy Rolls-Royce shop . . .

JACKIE: Buying a Rolls-Royce, yeh?

MUHAMMAD: Family go . . . t'gool, 'Okay, take one, two, three.' Y'gool, 'La. No now, soon. Bukra inshallah.' Elwāhid go, buy American car, is okay, t'gool, 'Okay, take car?' Y'gool, 'Okay, take car halheen, take car, shop, go.'[54]

JACKIE: Yeh . . . you take it with you, yeh?

FRANKIE: Oh – cash-and-carry?

JACKIE: It's fair enough, you know? I mean, if they're paying the money, you've got to come up with the goods.

IRVING: It's all right if you want a can of beans, isn't it? Some production line job. But a Rolls-Royce is craftsman built.

JACKIE: But you shouldn't 'ave to wait for it.

IRVING: 'Course you should.

JACKIE: No, not for that sort of money.

IRVING: You don't know what you're talking about.

JACKIE: It's bad sellin'.

FRANKIE: It's the same with clothes, Ir: you can't keep people hanging around till they're out of fashion.

JACKIE: That's right.

IRVING: But you don't get a decent suit off the peg, do you?

FRANKIE: Eh?

IRVING: You're a fine one to talk, anyway.

FRANKIE: What you talking about?

IRVING: Your clothes fall apart after five minutes.

FRANKIE: Don't be so bloody stupid.

IRVING: You're always taking them back.

JACKIE: It's bad business, I mean, you've got to fulfil your client's demands.

FRANKIE: That's right.

IRVING: That's all right if you want rubbish. If you want quality, you've got to be prepared to wait.

VERNON: If the client says he wants solid-gold door-handles with 'Abdullah' inscribed all over them, he's going to have to wait a couple of weeks for them to turn up, right?

IRVING: Right.

JACKIE: 'E's not called Abdullah, actually.

MUHAMMAD: Abdullah come here?

JACKIE: No, 'e's not comin' 'ere.

[*Pause.*]

FRANKIE [*to Muhammad*]: What exactly do you do, then?

MUHAMMAD [*to Jackie*]: Excuse?

JACKIE: He's a business man.

FRANKIE: Oh, yes?

JACKIE [*to Muhammad*]: You're in business.

MUHAMMAD [*to Frankie*]: Business, business.

JACKIE: Yeh, he's in oil, you know, Ver.

VERNON: Yeh.

MUHAMMAD: Er, business, London.

IRVING: Oh, buying up London, is he, eh?

JACKIE: Yeh, that's right.

[*Muhammad holds up his empty glass again.*]

FRANKIE: Oh!

IRVING: Come on! Chop-chop!

JACKIE [*getting up*]: It's all right, I'll get it.

IRVING [*to Vernon*]: Do your job, eh?

MUHAMMAD [*to Jackie*]: Is okay: barman make —

JACKIE [*taking the glass*]: No, no, it's all right, I'll get it.

VERNON: He does! He does! He thinks I'm the sodding barman, Jackie!

JACKIE: No, 'e doesn't, Ver, it's just that I told him that's what this was called, the bar, yeh?

IRVING [*following her to the bar*]: You know where it is, the orange, do you? Underneath. All right?

JACKIE: Yeh, I know.

VERNON: What're you doing, Irving? 'Course she knows where it is — she lives here, for Christ's sake. Get out!

IRVING: All right.

FRANKIE [to Muhammad]: Where are you staying?

MUHAMMAD: Excuse?

FRANKIE: Oh, dear . . .

VERNON: Does this character think he's staying here tonight, or what, Jackie?

JACKIE: Oh, no. No, he's just come back for a few drinks, you know? Just wanted to meet some English people, an' that.

VERNON: Just so long as we know, right?

FRANKIE: Where . . . are *you* . . . stay-ing . . . ?

MUHAMMAD: Okay?

FRANKIE: Eh?

MUHAMMAD: Okay.

> [*Muhammad takes Frankie's wrist and attempts to leave with her. She offers little resistance.*]

FRANKIE [*remotely enthusiastically*]: Oh!

IRVING ⎫   Here! What are you doing!
VERNON ⎬ [*together*]: What's he up to?
JACKIE ⎭   What's the matter?

IRVING: Here! Here, get your mitts off, right?

  MUHAMMAD [*to Irving*]: Excuse?

FRANKIE: It's all right, Irving, it's all right!

IRVING: She's mine, right? Mine.

MUHAMMAD: Ismāh-ly.[55] [*He sits down.*]

IRVING: Okay?

MUHAMMAD: Okay. [*To Jackie*] Make, er . . .

JACKIE: Yeh, it's all right, don't worry.

> [*Muhammad gestures to Jackie to sit back with him. She does.*]

  Yeh — don't worry.

FRANKIE: Where's he staying?

JACKIE: He's at the Royal Garden Hotel in Kensington, actually.

VERNON: Probably owns it, doesn't he?

JACKIE: Yeh, that's right.

IRVING: In oil, then, is he, eh?

JACKIE: Yeh, 'e is.

IRVING: Yeh — like a sardine, eh? [*He laughs uproariously.*]

VERNON: They own the Dorchester, don't they?

JACKIE: Yeh, they do. [*To Muhammad*] D'you know the Dorchester? D'you know, the Dorchester?

MUHAMMAD [*to Frankie*]: Excuse?

FRANKIE: DORCHESTER. No, he doesn't, no.

IRVING: How many oil-wells you got, then, eh? Oil-wells?

MUHAMMAD: Excuse?

JACKIE: 'T's your business.

MUHAMMAD: Business, business.

JACKIE: Oil.

IRVING: Oil-wells?

JACKIE: Yeh, it's his business, you know?

MUHAMMAD: Important.

JACKIE: Yeh ... oil.

IRVING: Oil.

FRANKIE: Oh, dear. Look, in the car ...

MUHAMMAD: Car. Many, many.

FRANKIE: Petrol?

MUHAMMAD: Petrol.

FRANKIE: Is *oil*.

MUHAMMAD: Oyel! Okay!

FRANKIE: You see – he understands if you're clear.

MUHAMMAD: Means, zēt.[56]

FRANKIE: Oh.

JACKIE: It's your family's business?

MUHAMMAD: In my country, is important; very, very.

IRVING: Yeh, you don't have to tell us.

JACKIE: Very profitable.

VERNON: You're not bloody kidding.

JACKIE: Very much big money.

VERNON: Costs a bloody fortune, doesn't it?

MUHAMMAD: Filhasa. Yamm Dhahrān ... oil ... ābar azzēt[57] ... [*He makes a romantic gesture to evoke expansive oil-fields with awe-inspiring monolithic oil-wells here and there.*] Ooooh!

FRANKIE: Oh, I say!

JACKIE: It's your family business?

IRVING: OPEC?

MUHAMMAD: OPEC, na'am.[58] Sheikh Yamani ...

IRVING: Sheikh Yam – Shake your money, shake your money, eh? Eh? [*Vernon and Irving laugh uproariously.*]

FRANKIE: Don't be so stupid, Irving.

MUHAMMAD: You know Sheikh Yamani?

IRVING: I don't know him, no.

JACKIE: No, 'e don't know 'im, listen; 't's your family business?

MUHAMMAD: Business, business.

JACKIE: In your country –

MUHAMMAD: Big business.

JACKIE: – your family's business . . .

MUHAMMAD: Family.

JACKIE: At home.

MUHAMMAD: Family.

JACKIE: Where you live.

MUHAMMAD: Family.

JACKIE: Business.

MUHAMMAD: Family business.

JACKIE: Yeh?

MUHAMMAD: Is sheep. [*His pronunciation is such that nobody gets it; indeed, it sounds distinctly like 'ship'.*]

FRANKIE: Eh?

JACKIE: Ship?

MUHAMMAD: Sheep.

FRANKIE ⎫ [*together*]: Oh – ships!
IRVING ⎭   Ships.

JACKIE: Yeh, 'e's in shipping, you know; is it oil-tankers, yeh? Yeh, it's oil-tankers.

MUHAMMAD: Import sheep.

JACKIE: Important, yeh, it's very important, yeh, a lot of big deals go on with that.

IRVING: Onassis we got here, then, have we?

JACKIE: 'T's right, yeh.

VERNON: He's a magnate.

MUHAMMAD: Import sheep, import camel. [*He pronounces the 'c' in 'camel' as in 'loch'.*]

JACKIE: 'T's imports, yeh?

MUHAMMAD: Import sheep.

FRANKIE: Oh, he imports ships.

JACKIE: Yeh, he buys oil-tankers, you know, an' that, Ver?

MUHAMMAD: Import sheep, import camel . . .

IRVING: Import camels?

JACKIE: No, he doesn't.

IRVING: That's what he said.

JACKIE: No, he didn't say that.

IRVING: He did

JACKIE: It must mean something else, yeh? Look: what, do you, import?

MUHAMMAD: Camel.

FRANKIE: Oh.

IRVING: There you are, you see, eh?

VERNON: He's a camel importer!

IRVING: They must be running out!

[*Vernon and Irving laugh uproariously.*]

JACKIE: Don't be stupid. [*To Muhammad*] Listen – listen; it's buying and selling?

MUHAMMAD: Buy, sell, camel. Many, many camel. He come, Australia.

FRANKIE: Eh?

VERNON: He imports camels from Australia!

FRANKIE: No, it's kangaroos!

JACKIE: No, it must mean something else in his language – look: you do business in Australia?

MUHAMMAD: Business, business.

JACKIE: Yeh. Yeh, he does deals over there.

MUHAMMAD: Import sheep, import camel –

IRVING: There you are?

MUHAMMAD: – import, em . . .

JACKIE: Is it oil?

MUHAMMAD: Is, eh . . .

JACKIE: You buy oil? Yeh, 'e buys oil, yeh. Is it oil-tankers? Yeh, it's oil-tankers.

MUHAMMAD: Er . . . sakhla[59] . . . [*He gestures vaguely.*]

FRANKIE: No . . .

MUHAMMAD: Is . . .

FRANKIE: He's trying to say something.

MUHAMMAD: Make, er . . . [*He mimes vaguely.*]

FRANKIE: Moving?

JACKIE: No, it's not moving, no.

MUHAMMAD: Make, er . . .

JACKIE: Is ships, yeh? Big ships on the sea? Yeh, they are big, you know?

MUHAMMAD: Sheep, big . . . sheep.

IRVING: Boxes?

JACKIE: No, it's not boxes.

IRVING: Crates?

JACKIE: Crates, yeh. You put stuff in crates?

VERNON: Bloody cargo, isn't it?

IRVING: 'Course it is.

JACKIE: Is it cargo – you know, ship's cargo?

MUHAMMAD: Sheep.

JACKIE: What sort of cargo is it?

MUHAMMAD: Sheep ma'a,⁶⁰ mm ... [*He mimes two horns.*]

FRANKIE: Oh, hats, is it? Hats?

JACKIE: No, no, it's not hats.

MUHAMMAD: Er, sheep ma'a – 'Baa!' [*He mimes a goat ramming a wall, one hand as the goat, the other as the wall.*]

FRANKIE: Oh, Christ!

JACKIE: No, don't understand.

MUHAMMAD: Is er, sheep, ma'a ... [*He mimes milking udders.*]

IRVING: Here – is it a book or a film?

FRANKIE: Please, Irving!

  [*Vernon and Irving laugh uproariously.*]

MUHAMMAD: Make, er ... [*He picks up the rug and uses it as a moving creature.*]

JACKIE: No, it's fur, yeh, he's in the fur trade.

FRANKIE: Oh, wildlife, is it?

VERNON: Here – don't do that with the bloody rug!

JACKIE: No, it's all right, Ver, 'e's just trying to explain.

VERNON: He doesn't have to rip the place apart, does he? God almighty.

JACKIE: No, well 'e wasn't; 'e was just showing you.

  [*Frankie helps Vernon to put the rug back; this develops into a brief surreptitious fondling session, which nobody else notices.*]

FRANKIE [*to Muhammad*]: Mind your feet.

JACKIE: You're in the fur trade?

MUHAMMAD: Goat. [*His pronunciation is such that they still don't get it.*]

JACKIE: Good.

FRANKIE [*moving Muhammad's feet*]: Good? Oh, he likes this.

MUHAMMAD: Is goat.

JACKIE: Is good? Is good fur, yeh?

MUHAMMAD [*holding up his empty glass*]: Where barman?

JACKIE: 'S the matter, d'you want another drink?

MUHAMMAD [*to Vernon*]: Ya – khooyi.⁶¹

JACKIE [*taking the glass*]: No, it's all right, I'll get it for you. [*She goes to the bar and pours another drink for Muhammad.*]

MUHAMMAD: Er, goat.

JACKIE: Yeh, good, yeh, good trade, you know? It's worth spending a few grand on a really good fur coat, you know, it's an investment, init, there's always goin' to be a demand for that sort of thing ...

IRVING: That's right.

JACKIE: It's like gold an' jewellery an' that, specially at the moment ...

IRVING: Yeh.

JACKIE: My dad got me my jacket you know for my twenty-first I mean it's only imitation oh no it's genuine fox you know but I mean 'e said if I go to interviews an' that I'm goin' to look a bit special you know a cut above the rest.

IRVING: Well, you want to make an impression.

JACKIE: That's right, yeh. Shows you've got the money to spend you know and money talks.

IRVING: Yeh.

JACKIE: My mum always 'ad a fur coat she 'ad this lovely astrakhan, my mum's funeral my auntie come down from Birmingham she 'ad this lovely short fur grey jacket on you know it looked really special really glamorous.

IRVING: Chic, isn't it?

JACKIE: It was a really foggy day.

IRVING: I've got a sheepskin rally coat.

JACKIE: Oh yeh well a lot of business men wear them you know yeh.

IRVING: Wrap it round you, pull the collar up, surprising.

JACKIE: Yeh, well you get these weirdos on telly an' that saying they shouldn't kill the animals but I mean let's face it it's only the very rich person that can afford a good mink you know so they can't kill that many animals, can they?

IRVING: Right.

MUHAMMAD: Goat.

JACKIE [giving Muhammad his drink]: Good? yeh, it's a good trade.

MUHAMMAD: Import goat.

JACKIE: Imports and exports, yeh, it's very good.

MUHAMMAD: Import goat, import camel.

IRVING: Import camel!

JACKIE: No, look, it's camel coats, yeh?

MUHAMMAD: Import sheep.

JACKIE: Yeh . . .

FRANKIE: Import ships, yes, we got that.

MUHAMMAD: Import sheep, import camel.

VERNON: Import ship, import camel!

MUHAMMAD: Is sheep, is camel, is goat.

VERNON: Is sheep, is camel, is goat!

   [Vernon and Irving laugh uproariously.]

IRVING: Goat, eh?

JACKIE: No – it isn't!

IRVING: Well – goatskins, eh?

JACKIE: No, it's not!!

IRVING: Goat, is it? Eh? [He mimes goat horns and makes goat noises.] Eh?
   [He laughs uproariously.]

MUHAMMAD: Goat. Er . . . is goat! GOAT!! [*He repeats his own goat mime and noises of earlier.*]

FRANKIE ⎫   Christ, it is goat!
IRVING   ⎬ [*together*]: Goat!
VERNON ⎪   It is goat!
JACKIE   ⎭   No!!!

MUHAMMAD: Is sheep. Sheep, meehh! Sheep, sheep, meeehh!

FRANKIE ⎫
IRVING   ⎬ [*together*]: Sheep!
VERNON ⎭

JACKIE: No!

MUHAMMAD ⎫
FRANKIE   ⎪
IRVING   ⎬ [*together*]: Is sheep, is camel, is goat!
VERNON   ⎭

JACKIE: No, it isn't!!

    [*Vernon and Irving are helpless with laughter and glee.*]

VERNON: I don't believe it – he's a bloody sheep farmer!

JACKIE: No, no, 'e's not! 'E's just got 'is animals mixed up. [*She throws herself on the floor and demonstrates with the rug.*] Look – it's mink, yeh? Leopard skin?

FRANKIE: No, it isn't, Jackie.

JACKIE: It is.

FRANKIE: It isn't – he imports sheep and camels and goats, he just said so.

JACKIE: Yes, but 'e don't know the words in English.

FRANKIE: He doesn't speak English.

JACKIE [*to Muhammad*]: Look? 'T's animals, yeh? It's fur?

MUHAMMAD: For. [*His pronunciation sounds like 'fur'.*]

JACKIE: What sort of animal is it?

MUHAMMAD: For Hajj.[62]

JACKIE: No, 'e don't understand. [*She gets up and moves away.*]

FRANKIE: Fur hedge, is it? Oi! A fur hedge?

MUHAMMAD: Hajj.

FRANKIE: Hedge?

MUHAMMAD: Na'am,[63] Hajj. For Hajj.

FRANKIE: Oh, hats? Fur hats?

JACKIE: No!

FRANKIE: You see, I said it was hats.

IRVING: No, they don't have fur hats in Arabia, do they?

JACKIE: No, that's right, they don't, no.

MUHAMMAD: For Hajj.

IRVING: Fur-hudge? Fudge? No, Turkish Delight, you have, eh?
    [*Vernon and Irving laugh uproariously.*]
MUHAMMAD: Hajj, Hajj!!
VERNON: Hedgehogs! Hedgehogs! He imports hedgehogs!
JACKIE: It's not funny, Ver — just leave 'im alone, will you?
MUHAMMAD: Is okay. Hadhoula Kuffar. Make er — mm addeen. Is
    okay. Ashrah-lahum, er ... I speak him; Allāhu 'aleemum bimā fi
    guloob innās.[64]
VERNON: Allahoo li-oggly oggly-wiggly!
IRVING: Yeh, we had one at home, the knob dropped off, eh?
    [*Vernon and Irving laugh uproariously.*]
MUHAMMAD: Er, Hajj, er go, er Mecca.
FRANKIE: Mocca?
MUHAMMAD: Go. Mecca.
FRANKIE: Oh, Mocha coffee is it?
MUHAMMAD: Coffee?
FRANKIE: Mm.
MUHAMMAD: Coffee-pot. Import coffee-pot.
FRANKIE: Oh, he imports coffee-pots.
JACKIE: No ...
MUHAMMAD: In, er, suq,[65] in Jiddha, is er, one, two, three coffee-pot,
    is carpet.
FRANKIE: Soup, coffee-pots, carpets ...
IRVING: Got a shop, have you? Shop?
FRANKIE: Shop?
MUHAMMAD: Shop, shop. Many. Okay ... Okay ... Hajj. Hajj is
    important, very, very. Is make, er Islam, make, er, Islam ...
IRVING: Islam?
MUHAMMAD: Make, er, Islam, go Mecca, er, go Mecca ...
VERNON: Mecca! He's talking about bloody Mecca!
FRANKIE: Oh, Mecca!
IRVING: They all go down the Locarno, don't they?
MUHAMMAD: Go Mecca ... Go Arafat ... Go Muzdalifah, go Mina,
    Mina is Id el Adha.[66]
    [*Irving and Vernon laugh uproariously.*]
MUHAMMAD: Excuse ... Mina is sheep –
FRANKIE
VERNON   } [*together*]: – is camel, is goat.
IRVING
FRANKIE: Yes ...
MUHAMMAD: Okay, Mina is sheep –

IRVING
VERNON
FRANKIE   }[*together*]: – is camel, is goat ...
MUHAMMAD

IRVING: Yes?

MUHAMMAD: Make, go ... [*He makes a throat-slitting gesture.*]

FRANKIE: Oh! Chop their heads off?

VERNON: Oh, do you?

IRVING: Slit their throats, eh? You got an abattoir?

MUHAMMAD: For Allah.

VERNON: For Allah?

MUHAMMAD: For Allah.

   [*Jackie sits at the dining-table, alone. She is very upset.*]

VERNON: Sheep and camel and your goats, you slit their throats for Allah
  – Oh, I see, you take them to Mecca ...

IRVING: Oh, I see ...

VERNON: Your sheep and camels and goats, you go to Mecca and
  sacrifice 'em for Allah! Very nice!

MUHAMMAD: So is sheep –

VERNON
IRVING
FRANKIE   }[*together*]: – is camel, is goat ...
MUHAMMAD

MUHAMMAD: – is suq[67] in Jiddha, is coffee-pot, is carpet ...

IRVING: For tourists, is it?

MUHAMMAD: Is family business.

FRANKIE: You see, he's got a shop, Jackie.

   [*Pause.*]

MUHAMMAD: Wa[68] umbrella.

FRANKIE: Eh?

MUHAMMAD: Umbrella.

FRANKIE: Umbrella?

IRVING: Rain a lot, does it?

MUHAMMAD: Is hot, like this like this like this, make Marwan come
  London, buy umbrella.

IRVING: Well, you've come to the right place, then.

MUHAMMAD: Important ...

IRVING: London ...

MUHAMMAD: London ...

IRVING: Best umbrellas in the world, you know.

MUHAMMAD: Umbrella. [*He holds up his empty glass.*]

FRANKIE [*taking his glass*]: Oh, he wants another one.

VERNON: Same again, Sabu?

>   [*Pause.*]

IRVING [*to Jackie*]: Takes all sorts, eh? [*He laughs uproariously.*]

MUHAMMAD [*to Jackie*]: Okay?

>   [*No reaction from Jackie. Pause.*]

FRANKIE: What's the matter with you?

IRVING: Eh?

MUHAMMAD [*to Jackie*]: Okay, I come now?

VERNON: How about you, Jackie? Drink?

JACKIE: No, I'm all right.

VERNON: Want a whisky?

JACKIE: No. Just going to powder me nose, actually.

>   [*Jackie exits to her room, hastily. A door closes, off.*
>   *Irving follows Jackie.*]

MUHAMMAD [*getting up*]: I come now?

VERNON [*giving Muhammad his glass*]: Here you are, Gungha Din – get
   that down you.

>   [*The door opens, off.*]

IRVING [*off*]: D'you want a whisky?

JACKIE [*off*]: No, I'm just putting some lipstick on, yeh?

>   [*The door closes, off, then opens again.*]

IRVING [*off*]: What's the matter? Are you all right?

JACKIE [*off*]: *Get out of my room, yeh?*

>   [*The door slams violently, off. Pause.*
>   *Irving enters.*]

VERNON: What are you up to, Irving?

IRVING: Nothing. What d'you mean?

>   [*Muhammad holds up his empty glass.*]

FRANKIE [*taking the glass*]: Finished, have you?

>   [*Muhammad goes into the hall.*]

MUHAMMAD [*as he goes*]: Where he go?

>   [*Muhammad exits towards Jackie's room.*]

IRVING [*following him into the hall*]: Here, where are you going?

>   [*Muhammad knocks on Jackie's door, off.*]

   You can't go in there.

>   [*The door opens, off.*]

JACKIE [*off*]: Stop following me about!!

>   [*Muhammad staggers backwards into view as Jackie pushes him hard.*]

IRVING: All right? Got the message?

>   [*The door closes, off.*]

VERNON: Irving!

IRVING: Look, it's not me! Now you keep out of there, right?

VERNON: What's going on? Are you all right, Jackie?

IRVING: Yeh, she's all right.

JACKIE [*off*]: I'm just trying to put me lipstick on, y'know?

VERNON: Come in here, the pair of you, you're as bad as each other. God almighty! Children!

MUHAMMAD [*muttering*]: Wallah[69] ... [*He closes the lounge door from the hall.*]

IRVING: Hey! [*He opens the door, and goes into the hall.*]

  [*Muhammad disappears towards Jackie's room, followed by Irving.*]

  [*Off*] Hey, Sambo: what're you standing there for, eh?

  [*Frankie closes the door.*]

MUHAMMAD [*off*]: Excuse?

IRVING [*off; quietly*]: You're not going in there, you know.

MUHAMMAD [*off; quietly*]: Excuse?

IRVING [*off; quietly*]: You just keep out, right?

  [*The short following dialogue overlaps with the preceding short passage, starting when Frankie closes the door.*]

FRANKIE: Come on, then: who is she?

VERNON: Who?

FRANKIE: Maggie.

VERNON: Maggie?

FRANKIE: Yes – Maggie.

VERNON: Maggie is an old friend of mine. She's separated from her husband, she's got a little kiddy called Wayne, who wears glasses, and happens to have a hole in his heart, and sometimes I take them out, for his benefit, right? Last weekend we went to the zoo. And there's nothing going on between me and Maggie.

FRANKIE: Well, that's not what I heard from Irving.

VERNON: Oh, Irving's got a very vivid imagination, hasn't he? I've only got to mention a girl's name, and he invents a whole bloody romance for me.

FRANKIE: But you could've phoned me, Ver; it's been three weeks.

VERNON: I told you, Frankie: I wanted to let the dust settle; right?

MUHAMMAD [*off*]: What her name?

IRVING [*off*]: Jackie.

MUHAMMAD [*off*]: Excuse?

IRVING [*off*]: Jackie.

MUHAMMAD [*off*]: Ja ... r ... k ...

IRVING [*off*]: That's her room, and you're not going in there.

MUHAMMAD [*off*]: Jah . . .

FRANKIE: Well, I don't know what to think. I really don't.

    [*Vernon embraces her from behind.*]

VERNON: You do believe me, don't you, Frankie? I wouldn't lie to you, you know that, don't you? Trust me, Frankie. You do trust me, don't you?

FRANKIE [*turning to him*]: Of course I trust you, Vernon.

    [*They kiss, standing behind the sofa.*
    Muhammad knocks on Jackie's door, off.]

IRVING [*off, to Muhammad*]: What're you doing?

    [*The door opens, off.*]

JACKIE [*off*]: Leave me alone, will you? It's my room, you know?

IRVING [*off*]: I've been trying to keep him out of there.

    [*Jackie, Irving and Muhammad enter.*
    Vernon immediately terminates the embrace by dropping Frankie backwards over the sofa.]

VERNON: For Christ's sake, Frankie! Mind the bloody sofa!

IRVING: What're you doing?

VERNON: She's sitting on the back of the sofa, and goes arse over tip.

    [*Frankie rushes out to the kitchen.*]

  God almighty! I wouldn't let her drive you home, Irving.

IRVING: What d'you mean?

VERNON: She's had too much. She's drunk.

IRVING [*going towards the door*]: Get out of the way, Sambo.

MUHAMMAD: Okay, make –

IRVING: All right!! All right!!

    [*Irving exits.*
    Muhammad closes the door behind Irving.]

VERNON [*tidying up*]: Look at the state of this – treating the place like a gymnasium, she's out of control.

JACKIE: What's the matter with her, Ver?

VERNON: She can't take her drink, Jackie. She's an alcoholic.

JACKIE: Oh, really?

VERNON: Mm.

JACKIE: Thought it was a bit funny you know when I come in; I wondered what was goin' on. [*She sits down.*]

    [*Irving and Frankie can be heard having a subdued row, off, in the kitchen.*]

MUHAMMAD: Is okay, I make him . . . er . . .

JACKIE: What's the matter?

MUHAMMAD: Excuse?

JACKIE: Just 'avin' a whisky – all right?

MUHAMMAD: La!⁷⁰

[*Irving enters.*]

IRVING: Well, I'm not driving.

[*He goes straight out again.*]

MUHAMMAD: Orange juice.

VERNON: You getting any bother, Jackie?

JACKIE: No, it's all right.

MUHAMMAD: Okay: Barman – orange juice.

VERNON: Tell him I'm not the sodding barman, Jackie!

JACKIE: No, it's all right, he knows that, Vernon – just go and sit down,
   yeh? Go and sit down!

MUHAMMAD: Okay. [*He gets hold of Jackie's arm.*]

JACKIE: Don't pull me!

VERNON: Hey!

JACKIE: 'T's all right, Ver, I can handle it.

MUHAMMAD [*patting the sofa*]: Okay, make . . .

JACKIE: Don't pat the seat, I'm not a servant.

MUHAMMAD: Make, er, make . . .

[*Irving enters.*]

VERNON: D'you want a brandy, Irv?

IRVING: Yes, please. In there.

VERNON: She's had too much, Irving.

IRVING: You don't have to tell me.

[*Muhammad gets up.*]

   She's not having any more, right?

VERNON: It's not up to me, Irving.

IRVING: Yeh, well, don't you give her any.

VERNON: She's your wife, Irving, she's your responsibility. You keep
   an eye on her. Right.

[*Muhammad makes some attempt to get Jackie up. The following overlaps
   the preceding few lines.*]

JACKIE: 'T's the matter?

MUHAMMAD: Okay . . .

JACKIE: Just go and sit down, yeh? Get off me!

MUHAMMAD: Is okay . . .

JACKIE: Just get off me, yeh?!!

IRVING: Oi! You keep your hands to yourself!

MUHAMMAD: Wallah⁷¹ . . .

VERNON: Come on, come on! Sit yourself down, have a little relax, and I'll get you an orange juice.

MUHAMMAD [*sitting down*]: Hadha kelb![72]

VERNON [*pouring Muhammad a drink*]: Oh, you don't have to tell me – I have to work with him!

IRVING: You taking his side now, are you? You want to learn some manners before you come over here.

MUHAMMAD: Ēsh hal warta![73]

IRVING: You all right?

JACKIE: Yeh. It's my stockings.

IRVING: Sure? [*Nearly touching her legs*] Not bruised, are you?

JACKIE: No, it's all right!

MOHAMMAD [*muttering*]: Hadhy haggety, hadheech haggety, killihin haggāty[74] . . .

IRVING: Diabolical liberty!

VERNON [*giving Muhammad his drink*]: Here you are.

MUHAMMAD: Minhu hādha?[75]

VERNON: I know!

IRVING: What are you driving at the moment?

JACKIE: Well, I haven't actually got a car at the moment.

IRVING: Haven't you?

JACKIE: No, well I can't really afford – well, I can afford it, we get taxis laid on at work an' that, you know, it's a perk of the job.

IRVING: Nice to have your own wheels, isn't it, though, be independent?

JACKIE: Yeh. Well, I'll probably get one later on.

IRVING: You don't want to go phoning taxis during the day, waiting for them to turn up.

JACKIE: Don't need one during the day. I work at night. I sleep during the day.

IRVING: Do you?

JACKIE: I'm more of a night person anyway, actually.

IRVING: What sort of car d'you fancy then, eh?

JACKIE: Dunno . . . I might get a sports-car . . .

IRVING: Yeh, I can just see you in a nice MGB, you know.

JACKIE: Oh, yeh, they're nice-looking cars.

IRVING: They are, yes; still, if you want one, you're going to have to move fast, 'cos they're going to be collectors' items soon.

VERNON: You trying to sell to Jackie, Irving? Moving in on my territory?

IRVING: First come, first served!

VERNON: No, you go ahead. I make it a rule, never to sell to friends.

JACKIE: No, that's right, actually, Vern.

IRVING: I'll do anyone a favour.

VERNON: No, no, if you sell to a friend, there's a fault in the product, they come back, complain, ends up on your bloody doorstep, that way you destroy a perfectly good relationship.

JACKIE: Yeh ...

IRVING: No problem – I keep business quite separate.

JACKIE: No, you can't, you know ... I've worked in selling, yeh, an' it don't pay to get involved in your prospects. 'T's bad business.

VERNON: Yeh.

IRVING: You can't say we're exactly involved, you and me, can you, eh?

JACKIE: I'm not saying that.

IRVING: Not yet, anyway. Eh? Chance'd be a fine thing, eh? [*He laughs uproariously.*]

   [*Muhammad lights a cigarette, and throws his match on the floor.*]
   Here, what're you doing?

VERNON: Hi, not on the carpet, you bloody cretin!

IRVING: You're not in the desert now, you know?

VERNON: Matches go in the ashtray – Ancient English Custom – compris?

IRVING: Go on, get back to your tent!

   [*Frankie enters eating a piece of melon and a buttered roll.*]

FRANKIE: What're you going on about now, Irving?

IRVING: What's the matter with you, then?

FRANKIE: There's nothing the matter with me – you're the one with the big mouth!

IRVING [*to Muhammad*]: You fat Arab!

FRANKIE: Oh, for Christ's sake, Irving!

IRVING: You drunken slut!

FRANKIE: You what?

IRVING: Mind where you're walking!

FRANKIE: Oh, shut up!

IRVING: Don't trip over the rug!

FRANKIE: I'm not listening, Irving! [*She sits next to Muhammad on the sofa.*]

IRVING: Here, watch it – you'll fall off the edge if you're not careful!

FRANKIE: It's going straight in one ear, and out the other, all right?

IRVING: Just watch it, right?

   [*Vernon exits to the kitchen.*]

MUHAMMAD: Hadha kelb.[76]

FRANKIE: Eh?

MUHAMMAD: Ey-wa, kelb ibn kelb![77]

FRANKIE: Yeh, I know, that's how I feel about him, too.

IRVING: Why don't you blow in his ear?

FRANKIE: Oh, shut up, Irving!!

[*Vernon enters with a dustpan, into which he empties the ashtrays.*]

VERNON: Christ almighty, Frankie; are you eating again?

FRANKIE: Yes, I am, Vernon, if it's all the same to you.

IRVING: She's got worms.

FRANKIE: Sod off, Irving!

VERNON: You've just had a five-course meal, for Christ's sake! Cost me forty-nine quid!

JACKIE: Oh, really? 'T's a lot of money, you know?

[*Vernon exits to the kitchen, followed by Irving.*]

IRVING [*off*]: Hullo, Mrs Mop's on the job, then, eh?

FRANKIE [*to Muhammad*]: Are you all right?

JACKIE: Yeh, 'e's all right.

FRANKIE: I wasn't asking you.

[*Pause.*
Irving enters.]

JACKIE: No, I was just telling you. [*To Irving*] What sort of car have you got at the moment?

IRVING: Metro HLE.

JACKIE: Oh, really? How long 'ave you 'ad it?

IRVING: Couple of months.

[*Vernon enters.*]

JACKIE: Oh, yeh? How's it goin'?

IRVING: Oh, really well.

JACKIE: Yeh?

IRVING: Lot of Driver-Satisfaction.

JACKIE: Oh, yeh? Not had any trouble with it?

IRVING: No – no; no, no.

VERNON: What d'you mean, no?

IRVING: Well, it's only the carburettor, you know, fifteen-minute job.

FRANKIE: Drives it too bloody fast, that's why.

IRVING: Chance'd be a fine thing – the North Circular's always jam-packed.

JACKIE: 'T's bad, though, if you've only had it a few months.

VERNON: No, no, Jackie – it's a first-rate motor.

JACKIE: Yeh, but you want reliability, don't you?

VERNON: No, all the road reports in the trade press are agreed: Car of the Decade.

IRVING: Without a doubt, it's the most economical car on the road in Europe today.

VERNON: Engineering-wise, it's a breakthrough.

IRVING: With the split-action rear seat, you've got really versatile loadability.

VERNON: You've got Small Car Manoeuvrability, Big Car Comfort.

JACKIE: It's nicely finished.

IRVING: Superbly so, yes.

JACKIE: You can't get them, can you? You've got to wait about six months or something.

IRVING: No, well, that's all down to the unions, isn't it?

JACKIE: 'T's right.

VERNON: We've just been feeling the shock-waves of industrial action; that's all cleared up now.

JACKIE: 'T's disgusting, you know. That's the trouble with this country.

IRVING: It's the Communists, you see.

JACKIE: 'T's right, yeh.

IRVING: They're behind the unions.

JACKIE: Yeh, yeh.

IRVING: If we got rid of the Communists, we'd all be much better off.

FRANKIE: Bloody Communists!

MUHAMMAD: Kumnis?

FRANKIE: Eh?

MUHAMMAD: Him?

FRANKIE: No, he's not a Communist, no!

IRVING: No!

JACKIE: No ... we get a lot of Communists in this country.

MUHAMMAD: No good!

JACKIE: No, that's right.

MUHAMMAD: In my country, no kumnis.

JACKIE: They don't have 'em, you know.

MUHAMMAD: Wallah. Hādhōla fitna. In many country is – Ghadafi fi Leebya, suf al Yemen wal'Arāq u Eerān. Wallah. Ash-Shāh al-meskeen. Ash Shāh –[78]

VERNON: The Shah, yeh.

MUHAMMAD: Hādhōla ashee'ay. Wallah. Ash-Shāh.[79] [He makes a throat-slitting gesture.]

IRVING: Yes, slit their throats – best thing for 'em.

FRANKIE: Quite right.

JACKIE: That's why it's a rich country, you know. It's like my job, there's no union in that, 't's much better.

IRVING: Really?

JACKIE: Anyone starts any trouble, that's it, they're out.

IRVING: Same with your job, isn't it, Frankie?

FRANKIE: Eh?

VERNON: No unions in your job, are there?

JACKIE: What d'you do?

IRVING: Sits on her backside all day.

FRANKIE: That's not true, Ir.

IRVING: No?

FRANKIE: I'm in-between jobs at the moment.

VERNON: You have been for the last five years, haven't you, Frankie?

IRVING: Seven years, actually.

FRANKIE: Six, if you must know.

JACKIE: That's why British firms've got a bad reputation. I mean, you don't drive a Metro, do you, Ver?

IRVING ⎫   He's got an Ital.
VERNON ⎬ [*together*]: I've got an Ital.

JACKIE: That's right, yeh.

VERNON: British car.

JACKIE: Oh? – Yeh, I know.

VERNON: More power than Metro – more oomph.

IRVING: Just that bit more poke, eh? [*He laughs uproariously.*]

FRANKIE: Please.

IRVING: More difficult to park, though, isn't it?

VERNON: I don't have any trouble parking, Irving.

IRVING: No, nor do I – I'll fit into any space, eh? The tighter the better!
[*He now has a spasm of uproarious laughter quite unprecedented in its length and its uncontrolled hysteria, not to mention its obscenity. A short pause, then . . .*] Oops! – Excuse me!
[*Irving exits hurriedly to the toilet.*
Pause. Muhammad holds up his empty glass.]

VERNON: Oh, here we go again – more shookra. [*He takes the glass and goes to the bar.*]

MUHAMMAD: Where . . . al kumnis?

FRANKIE: No, he's not a Communist, no!

MUHAMMAD: No good!
[*Pause. Vernon brings Muhammad his drink.*]

VERNON: Here y'are, Genghis. [*He tousles Muhammad's hair.*] All right?

FRANKIE: D'you want some more melon?

JACKIE: No, he's okay.

FRANKIE: I'm just asking him.

MUHAMMAD: What your name?

FRANKIE: Frances.

MUHAMMAD: Excuse?

FRANKIE: Frankie. Fran – kie.

MUHAMMAD: Frarn ... k.

FRANKIE: That's right.

MUHAMMAD [*indicating*]: Is Jar ... k.

FRANKIE: Mm. Would you like some melon?

JACKIE: 'E's probably had something to eat in the hotel.

FRANKIE: Well, he might be feeling a bit peckish by now, mightn't he? Melon?

MUHAMMAD: Melon. It mean 'hub-hub'. In my country, is mewa, for eat. Is big. Is good. Hub-hub.[80]

FRANKIE: Well, would you like some?

JACKIE: He's just tellin' you what it's called, that's all.

FRANKIE: Yes, I know that. [*To Muhammad*] Would you, like, some melon?

VERNON: Come on, Frankie – it's only a little bit of green skin – I'm sure you can manage that.

FRANKIE: Honestly, Vernon! [*To Muhammad*] I'll get you some, anyway.
   [*Frankie exits to the kitchen.*]

MUHAMMAD [*following her into the hall*]: I come now?

JACKIE [*following him to the door*]: No, that's all right. What's the matter?

MUHAMMAD [*not having seen where Frankie went*]: Where he go?

JACKIE: Where are you going?
   [*Muhammad wanders down the corridor.*]

VERNON: He's going to the toilet. Form a queue!
   [*Frankie enters, with a piece of melon and a spoon on a dish.*]

FRANKIE: Where is he, then?

VERNON: He's under the sofa, look – can't you see his little feet?

FRANKIE: Oh, for Christ's sake. [*Going into the hall*] Coo-eee!
   [*Frankie wanders off after Muhammad.*]

JACKIE: Are you all right, Ver?

VERNON: I'm all right, Jackie – how are you?

JACKIE: I'm all right. I'm a bit tired, actually.

VERNON: Yeh?

JACKIE: 'Ow old is she?

VERNON: She's got to be forty.

JACKIE: Yeh, she looks it, actually.[81]

VERNON: Mm.

JACKIE: 'E's a bit loud-mouthed, an' all, isn't 'e?

VERNON: You're not bloody kidding. He's like that at work, all day long – rabbit, rabbit.

JACKIE: Does 'e sell?

VERNON: No.

JACKIE: No, they don't, them blokes; I've seen 'em before, it's all talk, no action.

VERNON: He'll get the push before the end of the year.

JACKIE: Oh, really?

VERNON: Yup.

IRVING [off, in the loo]: What's going on?

VERNON: Want a whisky?

JACKIE: Yeh, all right.

IRVING [off]: Frankie!

FRANKIE [off]: Nothing!

IRVING [off]: What're you doing?

FRANKIE: [off]: I'm just giving him his melon.

IRVING [off]: Who?

FRANKIE [off]: Mo-hammed.

　　[Frankie enters, still with the bowl and melon.]

　Come on; come and have your melon – come on! Come on! Come on!

　　[Muhammad enters, with his jacket mostly off.]

JACKIE: What's the matter with him?

FRANKIE: Nothing.

JACKIE: Come and get your jacket on. Can you hold that, Ver? [She hands him her glass.] 'T's all right. I'll help you.

FRANKIE: I think he's a bit hot, actually.

JACKIE: Well, 'e doesn't want it 'anging off 'im, does 'e?

MUHAMMAD: Barman, is el kumnis, is, make, er, Fran for him, is Jack for him, kumnis make, er, is, make . . . [He slaps the sole of his foot with his hand.]

JACKIE: No, Mohammed, listen to me; listen to me – come and sit down, yeh?

FRANKIE: Come on, come and sit down with your melon. Come on.

JACKIE: Come and sit over here, yeh?

FRANKIE: No, he's all right here. Come on.

　　[Muhammed sits on the sofa with Frankie.]

MUHAMMAD [muttering]: Wallah hādhōla fitna. Fi kill mukān. Suf al Yemen wal 'Arāq u Eerān[82] . . .

FRANKIE: Here you are – melon.

JACKIE: No, 'e doesn't want that, actually.

FRANKIE: He might.

JACKIE: Yeh, he might not.

FRANKIE: Melon.

MUHAMMAD: What him?

FRANKIE: Melon.

JACKIE: Can I 'ave my whisky, Ver?

MUHAMMAD: Melon, mean, 'hub-hub'. In my country –

VERNON: Oh, shut up and eat your sodding melon!

[*Irving enters.*]

IRVING: Go on – get it down you; don't waste it! It doesn't grow on trees, does it, eh? [*He laughs uproariously.*]

VERNON: Here, Irving: see if he wants a nut on it.

IRVING: Eh?

VERNON: See if he wants a nut on his melon. [*He passes the nuts to Irving.*]

IRVING: Oh, yeh, look, you haven't got any garnish, have you? Here you are. [*He sprinkles peanuts on the melon.*]

FRANKIE ⎫   For Christ's sake, Irving, he's not a bloody monkey!

IRVING ⎬ [*together*]: You'll like these, they're your favourites.

JACKIE ⎭   Oh, no, look, leave him alone – you don't have nuts on melon.

MUHAMMAD: Wallah . . .

JACKIE: Are you all right?

MUHAMMAD: Shukran.[83]

JACKIE: What?

MUHAMMAD: Shukran.

JACKIE: Sugar, yeh? D'you want some sugar on it? [*She gets up.*]

VERNON: Shookra! He wants a drop of shookra!

IRVING: Give him some shookra on his nuts, eh?

MUHAMMAD [*getting up*]: I come now?

VERNON: I'll give him a drop of shookra.

JACKIE: Oh, no, don't be stupid, Ver, don't wind 'im up, you know?

VERNON: It's all right, Jackie, I'm only kidding.

[*Jackie exits to the kitchen.*
Vernon immediately pours whisky on the melon.]

FRANKIE: Jesus Christ! What a waste!

[*Irving laughs uproariously.*]

Dear, oh, dear!

IRVING: Go on, get it down you!

[*Jackie enters with the sugar-bowl.*]

JACKIE: Here y'are, 't's all right, I've got you some. Come and sit down, yeh?

MUHAMMAD [*going towards the door*]: Okay, Jack, make, er ... [*He gestures to Jackie to go with him.*]

IRVING: Go on! Go on!

VERNON: Leave her. Come and eat your melon. Where are you going? Come and eat your nice melon!

IRVING: Go on! Bye bye! Clear off! Go on! Off you go!

MUHAMMAD: Allah ykhalleek.[84] Al kumnis make –

IRVING: Here. Look. I am not a Communist. Right?

MUHAMMAD: Kumnis, kumnis make –

IRVING: I am not – listen to me, Sambo: I am not a Communist.

    [*Frankie wanders over to the bar and pours herself a drink.*]

MUHAMMAD: Kumnis!

VERNON: He is! He is! He is a Communist!

IRVING   ⎫   I am not a Communist!
VERNON ⎬ [*together*]: He is a Communist!
MUHAMMAD ⎭   Kumnis!

VERNON: Here, Irving! Irving! Look, your wife's having a drink, look!

    [*Irving rushes over to Frankie at the bar. Throughout the next passage Vernon laughs uproariously.*]

FRANKIE: You bloody sneak, Vernon Staines.

    [*Irving confiscates her glass.*]

  Give me my glass back!

IRVING: You're not having any more, right?

FRANKIE: All right. [*She grabs the whisky bottle.*] Then I'll have whisky.

IRVING [*taking the bottle*]: You will not!

FRANKIE: All right then. [*She grabs the vodka bottle.*] Vodka – I like vodka!

IRVING [*taking the bottle*]: You give me that.

FRANKIE: Give me my glass back, Irving!

IRVING: No.

FRANKIE: Come on, I'm not going to ask you again – give me my bloody glass back!

IRVING: You've had enough, right?

FRANKIE: Jesus Christ, Irving: give me my glass!

IRVING: Just get away!

FRANKIE: No.

IRVING: Look: you want a drink, get yourself an orange juice.

FRANKIE: I don't want bloody orange juice, I want a gin-and-tonic, now, come on, give me my glass back!

IRVING: You're not driving in this state.

FRANKIE: All right, then, we'll get a taxi, Okay? Now give me that glass.

IRVING: Oh, right, yeh, we'll get a taxi, okay – that's why we run two cars, isn't it? So's every time we go out, we get a taxi.

FRANKIE: I'm not going to ask you again!

IRVING: Right. Okay. Drink away, then. Go on. Help yourself.

FRANKIE: Dear, oh, dear.

IRVING: Okay, yeh: we'll get a taxi. I'm the one that's going to have to pay for it, aren't I?

FRANKIE: I don't mind – I'll pay for it.

IRVING: Oh, yes – what with?

FRANKIE: With my money, what d'you think?

IRVING: What money?

FRANKIE: The money I've got in my purse, Irving.

IRVING: Yeh – where d'you get that from, eh?

FRANKIE: Don't be so bloody mean.

IRVING: Why don't you try going out to work, eh?

FRANKIE: I don't call poncing around a bloody car showroom all day work, Irving.

[*Vernon finds this particularly amusing.*]

IRVING: Right, we're getting rid of your car.

FRANKIE: Bloody Scrooge.

IRVING: You only use it for going up to the end of the road, to the shops.

FRANKIE: Oh, sod off, Irving!

JACKIE: Charming!

IRVING [*to Muhammad*]: What's the matter with you, Sambo, eh? Had your eyeful? Go on, clear off!

VERNON: He's all right, Irving.

MUHAMMAD: Okay, khallās,[85] barman –

VERNON: Hey: I'm not a barman.

MUHAMMAD: Utrud. [*He gestures throwing Irving out.*] Utrud hadha. [*He makes a similar gesture.*] Halheen.[86] Okay, I speak ... this is Jack, girl, mm [*he gestures denoting himself*] this Fran, girl ... mm [*he makes a similar gesture*] al kumnis –

IRVING: Hey! Hey! I am not a Communist, right? I'm a Conservative, and proud of it! And I'll tell you something else for nothing ... [*Taking Frankie's wrist*] She is mine, right? Mine. My wife. My ... wife. Okay? [*He drops her wrist.*]

[*Pause.*]

MUHAMMAD: Wife?

IRVING: Wife.

MUHAMMAD: Fran, wife?

FRANKIE: Yes. Unfortunately.

MUHAMMAD: Wallah[87] ...
   [*Pause.*]
FRANKIE: Are you married, are you?
JACKIE: No, 'e's not.
FRANKIE: How do you know?
JACKIE: I know 'is friend, yeh, and 'e isn't.
FRANKIE: Well, let's ask him, shall we? Have you got a wife?
JACKIE: What's the matter, don't you believe me?
FRANKIE: *You*, got a *wife*?
   [*During the following speech, Muhammad is mocked and mimicked by
   Irving.*]
MUHAMMAD [*tutting*]: Hādha suāl mustaheel. Ana Areby. Mā lāzim tas'al
   an il-hareem! Mā lāzim tas'al an addeen! Hādha ihāna! Antum wukekeen,
   antum al Inglees! Ana Araby. Okay?[88]
JACKIE: All right?
MUHAMMAD: Okay – barman –
VERNON: Hey, let's clear this up, once and for all, you and me, shall we?
   I'm not a barman. Right? Understand?
MUHAMMAD: Orange juice.
VERNON: Listen, you ignorant bloody golliwog, what have you got in
   there, sawdust? I've just told you: I'm not the barman. I live here. This
   is my flat. This is my chair. My music centre. My television. My bar.
   My sofa. My lodger. My property. Right. Understand? Has it gone in?
   Good! Jesus Christ!
MUHAMMAD: Barman: taxi!
VERNON [*shouting*]: Listen! I'm not a barman! Repeat: not a barman!! You
   want to know what I do for a living? I'll tell you what I do for a living:
   I sell motor cars – you know what I mean? Cars? Vroom-vroom? Ey?
   You want to buy a car, I'll sell you a car, here you are – [*he picks up
   a brochure*] – Mini: a little car for a little man. Very appropriate! I'm
   a car salesman, I'm not a barman. [*He bangs Muhammad on the head with
   the rolled-up brochure.*] Boom-boom!!
MUHAMMAD [*moving towards the table*]: Jack: make taxi! Jack ... telefon
   taxi!
JACKIE: Don't hit me.
IRVING: Keep your hands to yourself.
MUHAMMAD: Jack – taxi!
JACKIE: Get off me, yeh?
IRVING [*assaulting Muhammad*]: How many more times have you got to
   be told, eh?!!!
MUHAMMAD: *Barman!!*

VERNON [*screaming*]: I'm not a barman!! I'm not a barman!! I'm not a barman!! I'm not a barman!! I'm not a barman!! I'm not a barman!! I'm not a barman!! I'm not a barman!! I'm not a sodding barman!!

MUHAMMAD [*shouting as Vernon screams*]: Allah! Sa'idoony![89]

VERNON: Jesus Christ!

[*Long pause.*]

MUHAMMAD: Okay. I make telephone taxi, ana asaweeha.[90] [*He puts the telephone on the table, and sits. He picks up the receiver. He flicks and pats the telephone, helplessly.*

Jackie gets up and goes over to him. He gestures for her to dial.]

JACKIE: Excuse me. Did you ask if you could use that?

[*Muhammad looks questioningly at her. Jackie puts the telephone back on the unit.*]

You don't just pick up people's phones without asking, you know? Costs money.

FRANKIE: Well, he's got plenty of that, hasn't he?

JACKIE: That's not the point. [*She sits down again.*]

[*Pause.*]

VERNON: No. I'd like to see him telephone for a taxi. Come on! Telephone for a taxi! Is good. Okay. Telephone taxi! [*He puts the telephone in front of Muhammad.*]

IRVING: Help yourself!

[*Jackie gets up and goes to the bar.*]

VERNON: Very good, Okay, telephone taxi!

IRVING: There you go – that's it.

MUHAMMAD: Okay?

VERNON: Okay.

[*Pause. Then Muhammad picks up the receiver, and puts it to his ear.*]

MUHAMMAD: Taxi?

[*Vernon and Irving laugh uproariously. Irving's mirth subsides reasonably soon, and he goes over to the bar, where Jackie is pouring herself a drink. But Vernon's laugh is long, loud, ugly and malicious. When it is finally over, there is a pause.*]

IRVING [*to Jackie*]: You all right?

JACKIE: Yeh. Just 'aving a whisky.

VERNON: How are you, Frankie? All right?

FRANKIE: Yes, thank you.

VERNON: Hey, d'you know what? If you weren't a married woman, I could fancy you. How are you, Jackie – all right?

JACKIE: Yeh, I'm all right; are you all right? [*She sits on the sofa.*]

VERNON: So-so.

IRVING [*to Frankie*]: You all right?

FRANKIE: Sod off!

JACKIE: Charming.
   [*Vernon laughs.*]

FRANKIE [*to Jackie*]: What are you staring at?
   [*Jackie stares Frankie out.*]

JACKIE: How long you been working at your place?

IRVING: Five years.

JACKIE: Oh, really, yeh, d'you like it?

IRVING: Oh, yeh.

JACKIE: What's the management like?

IRVING [*sitting next to her*]: Harold? Oh, well, he's retiring at the end of
   the year.

JACKIE: Oh, really?

IRVING: Yeh, not before time, either. [*He lights a cigarette.*]

JACKIE: Yeh? – 'e's a bit past it, yeh?

IRVING: He's still living in the nineteen-thirties, you know. Thinks it's
   all done by gentlemen's agreement.

JACKIE: Yeh; you can't do that, can you?

IRVING: He wants to move over – give a younger man a chance.

VERNON: You ought to apply for that, Irving. Put it in writing. Step up
   the ladder for you.

IRVING: Yeh, I might just do that. [*He flicks ash into the ashtray across
   Jackie.*]

FRANKIE: Oh, yeh – that'll be the day.

JACKIE: You wanna grab the opportunity – you know?

IRVING: You wanna grab everything while you can, don't you? [*He
   laughs uproariously, briefly.*]

JACKIE: D'you want the ashtray, yeh?

IRVING: I can reach.

JACKIE: You have it – it's going on my skirt. [*She passes the ashtray to him.*]

IRVING: Oh, right.

JACKIE: Well, if a bloke can't do 'is job, you've got to get rid of 'im,
   you know, you can't afford to carry passengers.

IRVING: He ought to retire early, really – give other people the opportunity, I mean, there's so much unemployment about today –

JACKIE: They don't look for jobs, half of them, do they?

IRVING: No – nation of layabouts we're breeding, aren't we?
   [*Muhammad is drinking the melon 'juice' with a spoon.*]

VERNON: Is good, yes, you like. Very, very good, Okay, shookra, very
   good, very good, me Tarzan, you Jane!

IRVING: Here, Sambo: when you've finished that, we've got a nice piece of steak for you!!

　　[*Vernon and Irving laugh uproariously.*]

FRANKIE: Oh, leave off, for Christ's sake! [*She goes and sits with Muhammad.*] Now then ... I want you to tell me all about your life in the desert.

JACKIE: Mind my skirt, yeh?

IRVING: I'll mind your skirt ...

JACKIE [*getting up*]: You want to tell him to watch what 'e's doing with 'is 'ands, Ver.

　　[*Jackie exits to the toilet.*]

VERNON: You been misbehaving, Irving?

IRVING: What?

FRANKIE: He's disgusting.

IRVING: Eh?

　　[*Pause.*]

VERNON [*to Muhammad*]: You want a drink, Sooty?

FRANKIE: Would you like another orange juice?

IRVING: I'll get him an orange juice.

VERNON: Thank you, Irving.

　　[*Irving goes to the bar, and pours Muhammad's drink. Unseen by the others, he adds brandy and gin to the orange juice as well as whisky. Pause.*]

VERNON: All right, are you? Happy now? Got yourself a little friend to talk to now, have you? That's nice!

IRVING: There we are. Drop of whisky.

FRANKIE: I'll take it.

IRVING: Hang on, dash of soda.

　　[*Frankie takes the drink to Muhammad. The toilet flushes, off.*]

　There you are, Sambo – that'll make your hair curl.

VERNON: What d'you give him, Irving?

IRVING: Orange juice.

FRANKIE: Here you are. Drink it up.

　　[*Irving goes out to the hall, and meets Jackie on her way back from the toilet.*]

JACKIE: What's the matter?

IRVING: Nothing.

JACKIE: Just goin' to powder me nose.

　　[*Jackie exits to her room, followed by Irving.*
　　Vernon pulls Frankie into a passionate embrace.]

IRVING [*off*]: This your room, is it?

JACKIE [*off*]: Yeh, can you do us a favour, and leave us?

IRVING [*off*]: Nice, isn't it?

JACKIE [*off*]: Yes, it is. All right?
   [*Jackie slams the door, off.*
   Irving comes back into the room.
   Vernon releases Frankie just in time.]
VERNON: Watch your step, Irving – right?
IRVING: I'm all right. You all right, Sambo, are you, eh? [*He laughs uproariously.*]
      [*Frankie adjusts her make-up.*
      Jackie enters.]
JACKIE [*under her breath*]: Cigarette ...
   [*She gets one out. Irving lights it for her.*]
   Thank you. [*She sits in the armchair.*]
   [*Vernon goes to the music centre. Irving hovers round Jackie. Pause.*]
IRVING: Got nice legs, haven't you?
VERNON: Jesus Christ!
FRANKIE: Irving!
IRVING: Well, she has, hasn't she? Eh?
JACKIE: What're you putting on, Vern?
VERNON: What d'you fancy, Jackie?
JACKIE [*joining Vernon*]: Oh, I dunno. Put some Barry Manilow on.
FRANKIE: Rod Stewart?
VERNON: Barry Manilow.
JACKIE: Yeh – I like 'im.
IRVING: He's a bit immature, though, isn't he?
JACKIE: Yeh, 'e's nice-looking, though.
   [*Vernon puts on the record. The music starts.*]
   Yeh, it's nice.
   [*Vernon and Frankie gravitate to the bar, and vaguely bop. Jackie returns to the armchair, and sits in it. Irving continues to hover around her. Muhammad stands up.*]
IRVING: Look, about this test drive ... we've got a blue MGB in the showroom –
JACKIE: No, I don't really want one at the moment.
IRVING: I could bring it round any time – we're only round the corner.
JACKIE: I 'aven't really got time, you know, I'm very busy in my line.
IRVING: Well, just give it a try – you're not under any obligation.
JACKIE: Yeh, I know that – it's no use trying to sell to me, you know – I'm an old hand at that game.
IRVING: What about Thursday?
JACKIE: Would you get me another whisky, yeh?
IRVING: Soda? Same again?

JACKIE: Yeh. Fifty-fifty.

[*Irving goes to the bar. Muhammad has been standing up for some time, and is now very drunk. He now lurches towards Jackie. She gets up. The others do not take any notice of this, or of what follows.*]

What's the matter? Come and sit down, yeh? Don't pull the furniture around! What're you doing?

[*Muhammad turns Jackie upside down, picks her up bodily, and bears her out of the room.*]

[*Calling*] Vernon !! Vernon!!

[*Vernon and Irving run to her rescue in the hall.*]

VERNON: Jesus Bloody Christ!

IRVING: Here – put her down.

JACKIE: Vern – get him off me!

IRVING: Get hold of her, right?

FRANKIE: Jesus Christ!

IRVING: You filthy Arab, you get off her!

[*Irving pulls Muhammad off Jackie, thrusting him so hard that he staggers backwards into Frankie's arms in the room.*]

JACKIE [*to Irving*]: Get off me.

IRVING [*to Jackie*]: All right, all right, all right.

[*Vernon goes to Frankie and Muhammad, who is hardly conscious.*]

[*Groping*] You want a hand up?

JACKIE: Look, sod off, will you? Vern!

IRVING: Don't you want a hand up?

JACKIE: Sod off! Vern!!

[*The following speech runs simultaneously with the preceding passage, and starts as soon as Vernon reaches Frankie and Muhammad, who is hardly conscious at this stage.*]

VERNON: What's going on? What're you playing at? What's your game, eh?

[*Vernon hears Jackie ('Sod off! Vern!!') and goes back to her rescue.*]

Irving! What're you up to?

IRVING: Just trying to pick her up.

VERNON: Get off her. You were having a bloody grope, weren't you?

IRVING: You're not going to leave her on the floor, are you?

VERNON: You've had your hands on her all night!

[*Irving goes to Frankie and Muhammad.*]

Are you all right, Jackie?

JACKIE: Just get 'im out of 'ere, Vern!

[*Throughout the preceding section, Frankie has been propping up the virtually unconscious Muhammad.*]

FRANKIE: It's all right. I've got you, don't worry. I've got you. Jesus
   Christ! What a weight.
   [*Following Vernon: 'You've had your hands on her all night!' Irving comes
   into the room and violently pulls Muhammad away from Frankie.*]
IRVING: You get off her!!
FRANKIE: Irving!!
VERNON: Mind that bar!
   [*Irving frog-marches Muhammad round the sofa.*]
IRVING: I'll have you, you Arab, you bastard!!
VERNON: Watch out, Irving – mind the glasses!!
   [*Irving throws Muhammad headlong on to the sofa, causing an ashtray to be
   thrown on to the floor, scattering its contents.*]
FRANKIE ⎫ [*together*]: Look what you've done, you stupid bugger!
VERNON ⎭   You slob, Irving!
   [*Vernon exits to the kitchen.*]
IRVING: You keep your filthy hands off my wife! [*To Frankie*] What were
   you doing, eh?
FRANKIE: Eh?
IRVING: I saw you!
FRANKIE: I wasn't doing anything!
IRVING: Rubbing your body up against him!
FRANKIE: Don't be so disgusting, Irving, for Christ's sake!
   [*Jackie comes into the room and sets about trying to find her cigarettes.*]
JACKIE [*under her breath*]: Cigarettes ...
   [*Vernon enters with the dustpan and brush.
   Muhammad has surfaced and tries to get hold of Jackie.*]
MUHAMMAD: Jack ...
JACKIE: Just get off me, yeh?
   [*Irving hears this, and proceeds to assault Muhammad.*]
VERNON [*to Muhammad*]: Hey! You! Get off her!
IRVING [*attempting to assault Muhammad*]: Get back! You get
   back!
VERNON [*intercepting*]: Irving!!
IRVING: I'll get you!! I'll do for you!!
VERNON: Get off, Irving! Keep out of it, for Christ's sake!!
   [*Muhammad staggers behind the sofa.*]
JACKIE: Ver! Ver, get him out of 'ere, I don't wannim 'ere!
VERNON: You brought him here, Jackie.
JACKIE: I didn't! I didn't!
VERNON: He's your friend, Jackie –
JACKIE: I don't wannim 'ere – I didn't!

VERNON: He's your responsibility, right – you brought him here. [*He turns off the music centre and resumes cleaning up.*]

[*The following dialogue runs simultaneously with the preceding passage, starting after Vernon's line 'Get off, Irving! Keep out of it, for Christ's sake!!'*]

FRANKIE: Leave off, for Christ's sake – Irving, leave him alone!!

IRVING: What's the matter with you, eh? You a wog-lover now, are you?

FRANKIE: For Christ's sake, Irving – don't be so bloody stupid! You gone bloody mad, or something?

IRVING: You slut!! You cow!!

FRANKIE: Jesus Christ, Irving, stop it, for God's sake!

IRVING [*shouting*]: Why don't you just suck him off, eh?

FRANKIE [*shouting*]: Oh, for Christ's sake, Irving, don't be so disgusting!!

IRVING [*shouting*]: Go on – get inside his trousers! We all know what you're after – why don't you just get on with it?

[*Muhammad appears from behind the sofa and vomits on it.*]

VERNON [*shouting*]: Oh, my God! You disgusting animal!!!

FRANKIE: Oo-ugh!

[*Vernon exits to the kitchen, fast.*]

IRVING: You've got a damned cheek! You did that on purpose, didn't you?

[*Vernon enters, fast, with a plastic washing-up bowl. Irving and Vernon put Muhammad's head in the bowl, and force him into a kneeling position on the floor with it.*]

VERNON: In there. In there. Good, in there, see, there, right?

[*During the following passage, Muhammad continues to vomit intermittently, but audibly.*]

IRVING: What a waste of booze!

VERNON: What d'you give him, Irving?

IRVING: Orange juice.

VERNON: What d'you put in it?

IRVING: Whisky.

VERNON: What else?

IRVING: You've been giving him whisky all night.

VERNON: He can take whisky, can't he? – that's his drink – he brought that bottle.

IRVING: No, they're not used to it – they can't hold it!

VERNON: What else, Irving?

IRVING: Nothing!

FRANKIE: Irving!

IRVING: You shut up!!

VERNON: What else, for Christ's sake?

IRVING: Brandy and gin.

VERNON ⎫   You ignorant twit –
FRANKIE ⎭ [*together*]: Jesus Christ, you stupid bugger!

VERNON: – you fucking moron – you're worse than him!

  [*Vernon exits to the kitchen.*]

FRANKIE: You bastard – what d'you think you're playing at? Eh?

IRVING: He would have thrown up, anyway.

FRANKIE: Don't be so bloody stupid!!

  [*Vernon enters.*]

JACKIE: Ver – can I have a whisky?

  [*Frankie goes to the phone and begins to dial.*]

IRVING: You put that down!

FRANKIE: Jesus Christ, Irving!

IRVING: You touch that phone, I'll wring your neck!!

FRANKIE [*backing away round the room*]: Don't you threaten me!!

IRVING: I'll do more than threaten you!

JACKIE: Please, Ver. Ver!

VERNON: What, Jackie?

JACKIE: Can I 'ave a whisky?

VERNON: He just poured you a whisky, didn't he?

JACKIE: I want you to pour me one.

VERNON: If you don't want that whisky, help yourself to another one from the bar, for Christ's sake!!

JACKIE: Please, Ver!

FRANKIE: You stay where you are! Don't you come near me!

IRVING: I wouldn't soil my hands!

FRANKIE: For Christ's sake, Irving! You've gone bloody daft – you've got a bloody screw loose!

IRVING: Why don't you sit down, eh? Take the weight off your feet?

  [*Muhammad makes another vague attempt to get hold of Jackie from his position on the floor.*]

MUHAMMAD: Make taxi!

JACKIE: Get off me!

IRVING [*going for Muhammad*]: You leave her alone!!

VERNON: Irving!

IRVING: All right, all right, Vernon – just watch him, eh?

VERNON: Keep out of it – mind your own business.

IRVING: Look – it is my business: he's been mauling my wife!

VERNON: Oh, shut up!

MUHAMMAD: Make taxi! Make taxi!

VERNON: Oh, Christ! He's going to be sick again. In there. In there, see. There, there, there, there. Right?

[*Frankie and Jackie edge out of the room.*]

MUHAMMAD: Make taxi! Make taxi! Make taxi! [*He starts to cry, but is not sick. Throughout the following speeches, he continues to cry and whimper 'Make taxi!'.*]

[*Frankie creeps back into the room.*]

IRVING: Oh, for God's sake! Why don't you grow up? You cry-baby! What's the matter? You homesick, or something?

FRANKIE: Jesus Christ, Irving!

IRVING: Here, Vernon, you got any sand? Sprinkle it round his feet, make him feel at home!

MUHAMMAD: Make taxi ... Allah, allah ...

VERNON: Irving, you really are a berk, aren't you?

[*Vernon exits to the kitchen.*
Frankie goes to Muhammad.]

FRANKIE: Oh, Christ! I can't bear seeing a man cry!

IRVING: You keep away from him!

FRANKIE [*shouting*]: You shut up!

IRVING [*seizing her*]: Don't you touch him!

FRANKIE: Leave me alone, Irving, for Christ's sake!

IRVING: You keep right away from him, right?!

FRANKIE: For Christ's sake, Irving, leave me!

IRVING: Just keep away!

FRANKIE: Just leave me alone!

IRVING: You slut!

FRANKIE: Oh, Jesus Christ!

IRVING [*shouting*]: I'll kill you!!

[*Vernon enters.*]

FRANKIE ⎫ [*together; shouting*]: Vernon!!
IRVING ⎭   I'll kill you!!

FRANKIE ⎫   Vernon!! Vernon!!
MUHAMMAD ⎬ [*together*]:   [*shouting*] Taxi! Taxi! Taxi!
VERNON   ⎭   [*almost inaudibly*] You all right, Jackie?

I'll get rid of them.

IRVING: Oh, yeh? Vernon? Vernon? Shout for Vernon! We all know about Vernon.

VERNON: What do you know about Vernon?

IRVING: I know about you two. I know you've been having it off.

VERNON: You what?!

IRVING: You've been having it off, haven't you?

VERNON: You must be bloody joking. Right. The party's over. Piss off!
[*Pause.*]

IRVING: Haven't you been having it off, then?

VERNON: Irving: I wouldn't stoop so low.

FRANKIE: *Oh!!*

VERNON: Come on. Chop-chop. Closing time. Get out, and take your
fat wife with you.

FRANKIE: Oh!

IRVING: Right: time to go home, is it?

VERNON: Time to go home.

IRVING: Okay. [*He throws Frankie's bag into her lap.*] Get your coat.

FRANKIE: You get my bloody coat!

IRVING: *You get your coat!*
[*He throws her on to the floor.*
She gets up, and goes out for her coat.]

IRVING: Right. Thanks, Vernon. It's been a nice evening. I'll see you
Monday, right?

VERNON: See you Monday, Irving.

IRVING: Give my love to Astrid.
[*Frankie enters with her coat.*]

FRANKIE: Come on, for Christ's sake!

IRVING: Where are you going?

FRANKIE: To get my cigarettes.
[*Frankie goes to the bar, where Vernon is; Irving goes into the dining area,*
where Jackie is.]

IRVING: I'll phone you in the week, Jackie, all right? [*He pinches her*
bottom.]

JACKIE [*under her breath*]: Get off!!
[*Irving laughs uproariously, then exits.*]

FRANKIE [*quietly*]: Are you going to phone me, Vern?

VERNON [*quietly*]: Call you Monday, Frankie.

FRANKIE [*quietly*]: Right.

IRVING [*off*]: Come on!

FRANKIE [*going towards the hall*]: I'm coming.
[*Frankie exits. Vernon follows her.*]

IRVING [*off*]: Have you got the keys?

FRANKIE [*off*]: 'Course I've got the bloody keys!

IRVING [*off*]: Well, I'm driving – right?

FRANKIE [*off*]: No, you're not!
[*The front door opens, off.*]

ACT II

153

IRVING [*off*]: Look, I'm doing the driving!
FRANKIE [*off*]: It's my car, Irving!
VERNON [*off*]: 'Bye, now! Safe journey!

[*The front door slams, off.*
Vernon enters.]

[*Muttering*] Jesus Christ!

[*Muhammad attempts to light a cigarette. Vernon takes the cigarette out of his mouth, and confiscates the matches.*]

Oh, no, you don't – not in your state, you'll set the bloody place on fire. [*He picks up the bowl.*] Keep an eye on him, Jackie.

[*Vernon exits to the toilet.*
Pause.]

MUHAMMAD: La. La La. La. Mā dām Muhammad ygooloon 'La'. Amma Ibraheem aw Marwan 'ala kaifhum! Lākin Muhammad 'La'! La. La. L'abbid. Roohu intum yam; Ibraheem aw Marwan ila London. Twannisu! Ishrabu! Dakhinu! Lākin Muhammad? La! Muhammad? Hadha kelb! Hadha h'marr! Hadha akmak! Ammar Bandar aw Turki aw Ahmad aw Selmaan aw Alawi aw Hisham 'ala kaifhum! Roohu intum ila Beirut aw Qaahirah. Twannisu[91] . . .

[*Jackie bolts over to the bar.*]

Jack? . . . Is Frank? . . . Is Jack? Okay, I speak . . . Okay? Okay. Okay, you speak wife. Is . . . I go Taif . . . is camel make . . . [*He makes an arm-ripping gesture.*] I go Abha, is make . . . [*He pauses.*] Allah. Allah. Allah. Is – is – is [*He pounds himself.*] Ya ba'ad galby.[92] [*He punches the sofa once.*] No . . . eh . . . speak . . . ya ba'ad galby! [*He punches the sofa twice.*]

JACKIE: Don't bang that settee!

[*Muhammad raises himself up, and makes a final tortuous attempt to communicate with Jackie: it is identifiable with clarity neither in English nor in Arabic. It builds to a painful climax, and then Muhammad collapses on the floor.*]

What's the matter with you? Get up on the settee? Get up, yeh? 'S the matter with you?

[*She tries to lift him on to the sofa, and fails, winding up on the floor with him, exhausted and fraught.*
Vernon enters.]

VERNON: What's going on, Jackie?
JACKIE: Just trying to get him on the settee.

[*Pause. Jackie kneels up. Vernon stands by her. He touches her hair.*]

I don't even know him. I know 'is friend, you know – he's really nice.
VERNON: You've got to be careful with these geezers. Can't trust them, can you?

JACKIE: I don't want him here!!

VERNON: You brought him here, Jackie. [*He moves away to the bar. He takes a swig of his drink.*] Right. Let's get this monkey on his feet. [*He goes to Muhammad.*] Come on. On your feet. Come on, get up. Get up. Wake up. [*He smacks Muhammad's face.*] Come on. Time to go home! On your feet! Come on! Get up! For Christ's sake. Come on! Christ; he's spark out, isn't he?

JACKIE: Mm. That settee all right, Ver?

VERNON: Suppose so.

JACKIE: If there's any sick-stains or anything on the carpet, Abdullah'll pay for it. Come out of 'is expenses.

VERNON: He'll pay for it himself.

JACKIE: Yeh, he's got the money.

VERNON: Where's he keep it?

JACKIE: In his trousers.

[*Vernon takes out the wad of money, and inspects it.*]

You wanna keep some of that, and pay for the damages.

VERNON: There's nothing damaged, is there? [*He puts the money back.*] It'll pay for his bloody taxi, anyway, won't it?

JACKIE: What you gonna do?

VERNON: Leave him.

JACKIE: If you stick him in a taxi, they can shove him off at the hotel.

VERNON: I can't stick him in a taxi – look at the size of him. I can't shift him down two flights of stairs.

JACKIE: You can't just leave 'im there.

VERNON: Yeh: let him sleep it off. Do him good.

[*Pause.*]

JACKIE: Ver ...

VERNON: What?

JACKIE: Can I have a whisky?

VERNON: What d'you want? Mine or his?

JACKIE: I don't want 'is!

[*Vernon pours the whisky. He picks up the water-jug.*]

Can I have soda?

[*He gives her soda. He puts her drink on the bar.*]

VERNON: There you are. [*He proceeds to empty ashtrays into the dustpan.*] Cost me a bloody fortune tonight. Those Gammons. They're gannets!

JACKIE: That bloke think you was up to something?

VERNON: What?

JACKIE: With 'is wife?

VERNON: Who? Irving?

JACKIE: Yeh.

VERNON: Yes, he did, didn't he?

JACKIE: Yeh.

VERNON: No way – d'you see her?

JACKIE: Yeh, I did.

VERNON: Yuk!

[*Vernon exits to the kitchen to put the dustpan away. He turns out the kitchen light and returns.*]

JACKIE: See what 'e did to me when 'e went?

VERNON: No, what d'e do?

JACKIE: Put 'is 'and up my skirt.

VERNON: Did he? Jesus Christ, there's something the matter with that guy, I tell you.

[*Vernon switches off the lamp on the bar, then the lamp on the wall-unit.*]

Right. I've had enough. I'm turning in. Get some shuteye. [*He stands near Jackie.*] Look at him. Quite sweet, isn't he?

[*Vernon draws Jackie to him. She is resistant at first, but only for a few moments. He kisses her rapaciously, and for quite a long time. When the kiss is over, she gasps. He still holds her in an embrace. She whimpers into his chest.*]

Why don't you stay with me tonight? That's your best bet. Then if he wakes up, you'll be all right.

JACKIE: I dunno ...

[*He releases her. He goes to the door.*]

VERNON: Think about it.

[*Vernon switches off the main light and exits to his room.*
Pause. Jackie goes to get one of her cigarettes. She lights one. Muhammad starts to move. Pause. Muhammad starts to snore. Jackie goes into the hall, closing the door behind her. She closes the other door.
Jackie exits.
The hall light goes out, and Vernon's door closes, off. Silence. Muhammad snores. The lights slowly fade to a Blackout.]

NOTES

1. No.
2. Forgive me.
3. Forgive me.
4. With.
5. And.
6. Those other girls.
7. Salim and Company.
8. No.
9. You don't understand.
10. With.
11. How much is it?
12. If Allah wills (God willing).
13. Toilet.
14. Jug of water.
15. Jug of water . . . by Allah (God Almighty).
16. I'll do it myself.
17. What a situation! What a situation! Anyway . . .
18. No.
19. This is an impossible question.
20. If Allah wills (in God's good time).
21. Strange.
22. Thank you.
23. Strange.
24. How much is it?
25. Yes. How much is it?
26. The money.
27. Donkey! Idiot! How could you make such a mistake? Forgive me.
28. Excellent!
29. More/faster.
30. What happens next?
31. Dance!
32. Dance for me!
33. Dance!
34. The lights.
35. Become naked (take all your clothes off/get undressed).
36. No – leave the lights off.
37. If it's you, the lights (since it's you, I'll allow the lights to stay on).
38. If Allah wills.
39. The lights.
40. It is the end (this is the giddy limit . . . this is just about as much as I can take).

41. What a situation.
42. Allah be praised (praise be to God).
43. Excellent! Okay, faster/more!
44. Okay, dance, dance for me, make, er make – okay, make, er dance, make, er okay, take er, okay, get undressed! Good! Okay! Dance! Dance for me! Clothes!
45. Get undressed.
46. Excellent.
47. Okay, faster/more, make, er – excellent!
48. Faster/more.
49. No.
50. With.
51. No.
52. Thank you.
53. One/a person.
54. Family go ... you say, 'Okay, take one, two, three.' He says, 'No. Not now soon. Tomorrow, God willing. One goes (to) buy American car, it's okay, you say, 'Okay, take car?' He says, 'Okay, take car right now, take car, shop, go.'
55. Forgive me.
56. Oil.
57. In the Eastern Province. Round Dhahran ... oil ... oil-fields.
58. Yes.
59. Goat.
60. With.
61. Hey – my friend.
62. (The Hajj is the Great Pilgrimage to Mecca. Every Muslim is expected to undertake the Hajj at least once in his life.)
63. Yes.
64. Is okay. They are unbelievers. Make er – mm – our religion. Is okay. I will explain to them, er ... I speak him; Allah is aware what is in people's hearts.
65. Market.
66. Go Mecca ... Go Arafat ... Go Muzdalifah, go Mina, Mina is the Feast of the Sacrifice.
67. Market in Jiddha.
68. And.
69. By Allah (God Almighty!).
70. No.
71. By Allah.
72. He is a dog!
73. What a situation!
74. This one's mine, that one's mine, all of them are mine ...
75. Who is this person?
76. He is a dog.

77. Absolutely – a dog – the son of a dog!
78. By Allah. They are a nuisance. In many country is – Ghadafi of Libya, look at Yemen and Iraq and Iran. By Allah. The Shah, the poor Shah –
79. Those Shi-ites. By Allah. The Shah.
80. Melon. It means 'water-melon'. In my country, is sweet, for eat. Is big. Is good. Water-melon.
81. (Frankie is, of course, much nearer thirty than forty.)
82. By Allah. They are a nuisance. Everywhere. Look at Yemen and Iraq and Iran.
83. Thank you.
84. Allah preserve you (may God preserve you from my wrath).
85. It is the end (see note 40).
86. Throw him out . . . Throw this person out . . . Right now.
87. By Allah.
88. This is an impossible question. I am an Arab. You shouldn't ask (an Arab) about his wife! You shouldn't ask (him) about his religion! It is rude! You are rude, you English! I am an Arab. Okay?
89. Help.
90. I'll do it myself.
91. No. No. No. No. If it's Muhammad, the answer is 'No'. As for Ibraheem and Marwan, they can do as they like! But Muhammad? 'No!' No. No. Absolutely not. Everybody else (can) go; Ibraheem and Marwan to London. Have a good time! Drink! Smoke! But Muhammad? No! Muhammad? He is a dog! He is a donkey! He is an idiot! As for Bandar and Turki and Ahmad and Selmaan and Alawi and Hisham, they can do whatever they like! Everybody go to Beirut and Cairo. Have a good time . . .
92. Oh, one after my heart (you are my ideal girl).

READ MORE IN PENGUIN

In every corner of the world, on every subject under the sun, Penguin represents quality and variety – the very best in publishing today.

For complete information about books available from Penguin – including Puffins, Penguin Classics and Arkana – and how to order them, write to us at the appropriate address below. Please note that for copyright reasons the selection of books varies from country to country.

In the United Kingdom: Please write to *Dept. EP, Penguin Books Ltd, Bath Road, Harmondsworth, West Drayton, Middlesex UB7 0DA*

In the United States: Please write to *Consumer Sales, Penguin USA, P.O. Box 999, Dept. 17109, Bergenfield, New Jersey 07621-0120.* VISA and MasterCard holders call 1-800-253-6476 to order Penguin titles

In Canada: Please write to *Penguin Books Canada Ltd, 10 Alcorn Avenue, Suite 300, Toronto, Ontario M4V 3B2*

In Australia: Please write to *Penguin Books Australia Ltd, P.O. Box 257, Ringwood, Victoria 3134*

In New Zealand: Please write to *Penguin Books (NZ) Ltd, Private Bag 102902, North Shore Mail Centre, Auckland 10*

In India: Please write to *Penguin Books India Pvt Ltd, 706 Eros Apartments, 56 Nehru Place, New Delhi 110 019*

In the Netherlands: Please write to *Penguin Books Netherlands bv, Postbus 3507, NL-1001 AH Amsterdam*

In Germany: Please write to *Penguin Books Deutschland GmbH, Metzlerstrasse 26, 60594 Frankfurt am Main*

In Spain: Please write to *Penguin Books S. A., Bravo Murillo 19, 1° B, 28015 Madrid*

In Italy: Please write to *Penguin Italia s.r.l., Via Felice Casati 20, I–20124 Milano*

In France: Please write to *Penguin France S. A., 17 rue Lejeune, F–31000 Toulouse*

In Japan: Please write to *Penguin Books Japan, Ishikiribashi Building, 2–5–4, Suido, Bunkyo-ku, Tokyo 112*

In South Africa: Please write to *Longman Penguin Southern Africa (Pty) Ltd, Private Bag X08, Bertsham 2013*

READ MORE IN PENGUIN

A SELECTION OF PLAYS

Edward Albee	**Who's Afraid of Virginia Woolf?**
Alan Ayckbourn	**Joking Apart and Other Plays**
Dermot Bolger	**A Dublin Quartet**
Bertolt Brecht	**Parables for the Theatre**
Anton Chekhov	**Plays (The Cherry Orchard/Three Sisters/ Ivanov//The Seagull/Uncle Vania)**
Henrik Ibsen	**A Doll's House/League of Youth/Lady from the Sea**
Eugène Ionesco	**Rhinoceros/The Chairs/The Lesson**
Ben Jonson	**Three Comedies (Volpone/The Alchemist/ Bartholomew Fair)**
D. H. Lawrence	**Three Plays (The Collier's Friday Night/ The Daughter-in-Law/The Widowing of Mrs Holroyd)**
Arthur Miller	**Death of a Salesman**
John Mortimer	**A Voyage Round My Father/What Shall We Tell Caroline?/The Dock Brief**
J. B. Priestley	**Time and the Conways/I Have Been Here Before/An Inspector/The Linden Tree**
Peter Shaffer	**Lettice and Lovage/Yonadab**
Bernard Shaw	**Plays Pleasant (Arms and the Man/ Candida /The Man of Destiny/You Never Can Tell)**
Sophocles	**Three Theban Plays (Oedipus the King/ Antigone/ Oedipus at Colonus)**
Wendy Wasserstein	**The Heidi Chronicles and Other Plays**
Keith Waterhouse	**Jeffrey Bernard is Unwell and Other Plays**
Arnold Wesker	**Plays, Volume 1: The Wesker Trilogy (Chicken Soup with Barley/Roots/I'm Talking about Jerusalem)**
Oscar Wilde	**The Importance of Being Earnest and Other Plays**
Thornton Wilder	**Our Town/The Skin of Our Teeth/The Matchmaker**
Tennessee Williams	**Cat on a Hot Tin Roof/The Milk Train Doesn't Stop Here Anymore/The Night of the Iguana**